HEART

OF

WORSHIP

BIBLICAL ORIGINS OF CONTEMPORARY WORSHIP

By
LeAnne Freesemann

Restoring Word Publishing
Broken Arrow, Oklahoma 74012
www.restoringword.com

Unless otherwise indicated, all scripture is taken from New King James Version. Copyright ©1982 by Thomas Nelson, Inc. Used by permission. All rights reserved.

Ordering Information:
Quantity sales. Special discounts are available on quantity purchases by corporations, associations, and others. For details, contact the "Special Sales Department" at the address above.

Book Layout ©2017 BookDesignTemplates.com

Born for More / LeAnne Freesemann. —1st ed.
ISBN **978-1-7324766-1-5**

LeAnne Freesemann takes us on a journey of discovery of what it means to be a true worshiper. With a perfect blend of personal examples and sound biblical principles, this book will help set a firm foundation in your understanding of worship and how to develop the heart of a worshiper. Whether you are a seasoned worship leader or just starting to learn about worship, this book will surely become a go-to resource!

~Dr. Edwin Miranda

Acknowledgements

This book is was in my spirit for many years, but, it took the encouragement of friends and family to sit down and begin to write it.

Carol Worley was that friend who said, "LeAnne, you have something to say and you need to write it now." Without her encouragement and willingness to brainstorm and edit, it would not have happened.

My best friend and covenant life partner Grant Freesemann – thank you for taking care of me so I can care for others. You make my crazy life possible and your patience with me is appreciated. I love you.

Jenava and Josiah, you are my greatest blessings from heaven. Thank you for loving me and surviving those years of being my students. I am honored to be your mother, and I am thankful for your love and encouragement.

Ramona, you are the woman of God every person wants to be. Thank you for your love and support.

Diana Collins, your wisdom on this project was priceless. Thank you for your editing eye and encouragement.

Dan Tetrault and DTCreative, you always go far beyond what I could ever imagine with your design ideas. Your cover design was just what I wanted. Thank you!

Dad, your unconditional support is why I hung in there and didn't give up. Thank you for helping me and our little family in so many ways.

Merle and Joyce Wagner are our spiritual parents and they saw the call of God on us and supported us when no one else did. Thank you! You gave us courage and strength and taught us what it meant to give unconditionally. Our heavenly reward for obedience is yours as well.

Contents

Dedication

For my mother Nancy Conway Luikart.

Mom had a gift from God and she knew it.
She didn't understand the presence of God that came upon her when she sang.
But when she sang, you could feel it.

God's presence could be heard in her voice, and I got to hear it on a daily basis.
I am so thankful for her example and her life.

She never gave up on me.
She stayed with me and supported me through those long, lost years.
She is in Heaven now.
This biblical worship book is dedicated in her honor.
She taught me and countless others about the presence of God.

I want to thank all of my former students who helped formulate this book.
Run with the call of God.
The nations are awaiting you.

CHAPTER 1

Worship

> *"Above all sing spiritually. Have an eye to God in every word you sing.*
> *Aim at pleasing Him more than yourself, or any other creature.*
> *In order to do this, attend strictly to the sense of what you sing, and see that*
> *your heart is not carried away with the sound, but offered to God continually; so*
> *shall your singing be such as the Lord will approve here, and reward you*
> *when he cometh in the clouds of heaven."*
>
> —*John Wesley*

A large black baby grand piano filled the far end of my living room in my home in Sioux City, Iowa. This large instrument filled my childhood home with music. When my mother sat down to sing, the presence of God would fill our home. I remember my mother's voice as huge. She always knew that she had a gift from God. My grandmother and my great grandmother before her all were singers in the local Methodist Church. Mom sang for congressmen and senators as well as presidents and other dignitaries. She knew her voice was a gift from God and that it was what made her special. When she started singing high notes, you could hear the crystal vibrating in the dining room a few feet away. The presence of God was all over her voice. And I grew up hearing that presence on a daily basis. It was a big gift in the natural, but more than that I could sense the presence of God on her singing voice.

Sensing the supernatural presence of God on vocalists is something that is spiritually discerned. It isn't something that can be taught from a textbook. It has nothing to do with style. It has everything to do with the heart of the person doing the singing.

Colossians 3:16 tells us that the Word of God dwells in us richly, "teaching and admonishing one another in wisdom, singing songs and hymns and spiritual songs, with thankfulness in your hearts to God." When you sing, you are letting the Word of God come out of your mouth. You are releasing Scripture over your situation.

Ephesians 5:18 tells us that we are to "sing psalms, hymns, and spiritual songs, singing and making melody in our heart to the Lord." Music is an intimate and personal thing between the musician and God. God gave the gift, and He enjoys hearing that gift release praise and worship back to Him.

That's why it's so important that we're careful with lyrics. The lyrics in our praise and worship songs are the theology in the church. The lyrics in those songs unite congregations in their beliefs. We teach our congregations our beliefs by the lyrics that are in our songs. What you sing and how you sing is advertising to the world what you believe. Have you ever left the church service with a song in your head, and you find yourself singing it all week long? I do. I love it when I go home and I'm still singing worship songs in my head after the service.

It's take-home theology. Most praise and worship songs run three to five minutes. They are easy to memorize, and they amplify important biblical truths from the Word of God. The song I'm currently hearing in my head is often the one the Holy Spirit is using to encourage me to bring me strength.

Singing is encouraging. When you sing with others, you build up not only yourself but others as well. Let's face it: life is not always easy. So, when a group of believers come together and sing songs, they speak life to each other.

One of my favorite administrators at my school used to smuggle Bibles behind the Iron Curtain. He told me stories of how the believers met in secret locations so he could hand them Bibles. Everyone arrived at different times. They left at staggered times so that officials in those countries could not figure out that they were holding secret meetings. Once everyone was together, they sang psalms and hymns quietly. They sang low and softly because they were afraid of being heard. He often told me it was the most beautiful praise and worship he had ever heard. It was heartfelt and sincere. They could have all been thrown into prison for singing about their love of God. I've never forgotten that story because it always reminds me that that's what real praise and worship is. It comes from the heart. It's not about a decent sound check for the best musical equipment. It's always about what comes out of the heart of the believer who is singing it. It will breathe life into those around them that hear it.

When you go back and study church history, it becomes obvious what the Church was going through by looking at the lyrics of their songs. Whether it's Martin Luther or John Wesley, we can learn about the Church in the history of the body of Christ. Many of the songs written hundreds of years ago are still being sung today.

I recently had the opportunity to attend a church service up in Iowa where the pastor had done an amazing arrangement of "Be thou my Vision," an Irish tune sung hundreds of years ago. It opened with a powerful trumpet solo and to this day it is one of my favorites. The opening lines to that hymn still resonate in my spirit when I sing it now.

Many songs are truly timeless. "Amazing Grace" is one example. My husband did prison ministry for seven years, and there wasn't one prison that didn't love to sing, "Amazing Grace, how sweet the sound, that saved a wretch like me." That hymn still touches our hearts today. Ephesians 5:19 says,

> *...speaking to one another in psalms and hymns and spiritual songs, singing and making melody in your heart to the Lord....*

Clearly, Ephesians 5:19 tells us to address each other with the songs that come out of our mouths. According to the Scripture, we're to make melody in our hearts and to God. When we make melody in our hearts and to God, believers around us hear it as well, and they are strengthened.

When we sing as a group or as a congregation, we are all confessing the Word of God together. God dwells in the praises of His people. If you want to know where God is—where He can be felt—just go to an outstanding praise and worship service. Wait for that section in the worship where it gets quiet and just the voices are singing to God. That's where God dwells. That's where his presence is felt. And that is from where his power manifests.

Musicians have the capacity to open up the spirit realm. They do it by speaking and singing life into the congregation and empowering the congregation to worship God. But when the worship band is finally out of the way and the congregation can see nothing but Jesus, that's where God is.

Psalm 22:3
But You are holy, Enthroned in the praises of Israel.

Psalm 145:18
18 The LORD is near to all who call upon Him,
To all who call upon Him in truth.

Psalm 105:1-2
1 Oh, give thanks to the LORD!
Call upon His name; Make known His deeds among the peoples!
2 Sing to Him, sing Psalms to Him; Talk of all His wondrous works!

I love this portion of Scripture out of Psalms Chapter 105. It tells us that when we sing, we're actually bragging about God's goodness and His greatness.

Have you ever thought about why we sing at the beginning of our church services? Music is God's calling card. It is evangelistic. It draws in unbelievers as well as believers. The better the music is, the more likely the unbelievers will stay and pay attention. If we're passionate about winning the lost to Christ—especially in this generation that is spoon fed music from the iPods and iPhones—we have to make sure that we want music in the House of God that is of a certain caliber. It has to be excellent.

The Levitical priests in the Old Testament lived off sacrifices that people brought to the temple. In the same way, today's musicians should live off of offerings that come into the local church. They should be able to sustain themselves from the offerings that are brought to the ouse of God. Musicians in the local church should be paid.

Music has spiritual power, and when you sing and worship God, the effect is like lighting a candle in the darkness. When a candle is lit in a dark room, the darkness must go. The light from that candle illuminates the entire room.

That's what we do when we sing and worship God. We bring light into darkness. The highest form of spiritual warfare is done by the musicians. Musicians have the capacity to create sounds that make darkness flee. That's why any great musician will tell you it's all about tone and the heart.

Colossians 3:15-16
15 And let the peace of God rule in your hearts, to the which also ye are called in one body; and be ye thankful. 16 Let the word of Christ dwell in you richly in all wisdom; teaching and admonishing one another in psalms and hymns and spiritual songs, singing with grace in your hearts to the Lord.

When you sing and worship God from your heart, whether it's in the church service or listening to the Internet or any other kind of musical device, you bring God's presence and His Word into that situation. You're speaking light and life into yourself as you worship. As you sing to Him, you're inviting Him into every trial and tribulation in your life and doing so keeps you connected to God.

Example upon example exist in the Bible where we see vocal music. Moses had a song that he sang in Exodus 15. In this portion of Scripture, he's describing the great deliverance from the bondage of the Egyptians. Later in the chapter, we see Miriam, the prophetess, take a tambourine in her hand, and she and the ladies went out and sang praise to the Lord and danced after the victory at the Red Sea. In Numbers 21, Israel sang a song to the well in the desert. To find water in the middle of a dry place would've been a huge miracle. We also see the importance of the voice in the Book of Joshua, Chapter Six. When the priests blew the rams' horns and trumpets and then shouted, the walls came tumbling down in Jericho. Deborah was an important judge to the Israeli people who sang a song of praise to God.

It always makes me wonder which leaders today are worshiping God and thanking him for their victories. Recently a man campaigned for the United States Senate where praise and worship music came forth at his victory rally.

When the temple of Solomon was dedicated, a singer sang an important part of that dedication. One of my favorite portions of Scripture comes from Second Chronicles, Chapter 20. King Jehoshaphat used the ministry of the singers to lead the army against the Moabites and Ammonites. The singers went ahead of the army. When they worshiped and sang, they brought the presence of the Lord. Their God gave them favor in battle.

King Hezekiah also knew the importance of singing. In Second Chronicles 29, he led the nation of Israel and the great awakening. King Josiah revived the ministry of singers during his reign, and the priestly scribe Ezra had the singers minister when the foundation of the Temple was laid when they came back out of Babylon. The Levites wore their robes, and sang, and played instruments. Both men and women sang during this important dedication in Ezra 2 and 3. When Nehemiah went back to rebuild the walls of Jerusalem in Chapter 12 of the Book of Nehemiah, the singers sang at the dedication. Solomon, the son of King David, was also musically talented. He wrote hundreds of songs, and they are recorded for us today in the Song of Songs. When King David was reigning in Israel, it was a form of golden era in Israel's history. During this important historical reign, music and singing were featured. King David knew how to celebrate with song. In Isaiah 16:10, during the harvest, Israel sang as they trod out the grapes, producing new wine. Then, in Psalms 136 and Psalms 24, the singing done by the Hebrew nation was antiphonal: a part was sung, and then a response followed. Or, people would respond with a phrase or a song. Even today, in our contemporary services, there are verses and choruses that believers love to sing, such as "Amazing Grace."

Numerous teachers and conference speakers today teach on spiritual warfare. They can give you different prayer techniques, such as binding and loosing. They can teach you prayer strategies and Scriptures to pray. All that is wonderful and valid. If, however, you really want to defeat the enemy, just begin to lift God up and sing to Him from your heart in the middle of your battle and the middle of your pain, and you will see God move. Over the years I've learned not to be so consumed with the darkness or the battle, but to focus on lighting my candle in the darkness.

Singing is something that you must do physically. You have to open your mouth and make sound. Some people are natural-born singers, and some are not. It doesn't have anything to do with your talent; it really has to do with your heart. This isn't to say singing should not be done in excellence, but sometimes the most off-pitch singing from a suffering believer gives God more honor and glory than from a talented vocalist.

When you sing, you glorify God. Just think about it: you were born to sing. You are born with the musical instrument built into your body. Every person has that instrument. It's vitally important for you learn to protect it. You don't want to scream or yell or destroy it. Singing has a special way of bringing your heart, your soul, your mind, and all of your strengths together to focus entirely on God. It's your mind and your body working together to glorify Him. That also includes when you play a musical instrument. Every part of your being is actively glorifying Jesus.

When I come home from leading praise and worship, I'm tired mentally and physically. My hands and my back may hurt, but my spirit man is so happy and my mind is so peaceful that I always get my best sleep after I lead praise and worship.

I love that portion of Scripture from Psalm 150:6 that says,

"Let everything that has breath praise the Lord."

When you were born, God breathed His life into you. As long as you are living, you are breathing. Your breath and your life are connected. You can't live without your breath.

Well, you can't sing without your breath either. Breathing and glorifying God go together. Skilled vocalists learn how to control their air; so, they spend a lot of time doing aerobic exercises to build up breath and air support so that they can sing on pitch. These are natural things that we do to be excellent singers. When I do it, I'm also acutely aware that when I breathe, I am alive. That breath was given to me as a gift from God. Every time I breathe in air to sing or to speak, those gifts come from God.

All instruments have sound generators. If it's a stringed instrument, then the resonator is the body of the instrument. As vocalists, our resonators are our physical bodies, and our resonators don't work well without air. Air passes through the vocal cords, and the air that comes out of your lungs into those vocal cords gives you the ability to create sound. That sound is what the Holy Spirit can use to minister to others. That sound can release the supernatural. That sound can prophesy and bring healing into broken bodies, minds, and hearts.

I've always felt that our ministry title should be Prophetic Sound. Back in the 90s, that's what Grant really wanted to call our ministry. We are prophetic and we create sounds for the King. Of course, a lot of people don't understand that. So, we named our ministry Restoring Word. Grant works in the auto body industry: he takes damaged things and rebuilds them. The Holy Spirit does this as well in the lives of believers who have been damaged or destroyed by the attacks of the enemy. A prophetic word given at the right time and in the right manner can restore that which has been destroyed or broken. Your human speaking voice and singing voice allow Gods spirit to be released. Prophetic words from heaven can make a believer whole again. I passionately believe in the power of spirit generated sound in the atmosphere through prophetic words and songs.

Singing is incredibly important in the Bible. In fact, there are specific vocalists that are mentioned in the Old Testament. They had assigned singing responsibilities in the temple. They were so important that their names are listed in Scripture, and we say their names even to this day. The chief musician was assigned. His name was Chenaniah, and he had three assistants.

1 Chronicles 15:22
Chenaniah, leader of the Levites, was instructor in charge of the music,
because he was skillful....

There are many Old Testament studies that relate to modern-day praise and worship leaders. One of the most interesting one is the story of the Ark of the covenant. The Ark was an important symbol of worship that was housed in a tent in the tabernacle of Moses. The entire study of the tabernacle of Moses is important because it tells us how to get into the presence of God by following each of the stations in the tabernacle. I plan on covering that in another chapter. It is interesting that the Levites who carried the Ark of the covenant, which housed the presence of God on earth, carried this holy box on their shoulders.

When I think of the shoulder, I think of something that carries weight or has a lot of responsibility. The shoulder is symbolic of the government and the support and strength of the leader. I love that portion in the Hallelujah chorus that Humble wrote: "And the government shall be upon his shoulders." In the Levitical offerings, the animals' shoulders were a special portion given to the ministers as part of the sacrifices. And in First Chronicles 15, the garment that the high priest wore carried the names of the tribes on their hearts, but they were attached to something up on their shoulders.

All of this is symbolic of the fact that there is a structure in the government and an order within the Church, and those that are called to minister are going to carry the weight of that responsibility on their shoulders. It's also interesting to note that God did not permit any Israelites to run around with the Ark on their shoulders, but only those that were ordained to do so had that honor. God placed the government of his Church on the shoulders of those whom he called, and equipped, and ordained for that responsibility.

If you are involved in praise and worship, you understand the meaning of carrying the anointing. The presence of God, or the anointing of God, is within you, but at times, when you're leading worship, it will also come upon you in a heavier manner. When I was studying the Old Testament, this jumped out at me. The Levites were set aside to minister to the Lord in the tabernacle. They had to carry this holy box in the way the Lord wanted it to be carried. It wasn't something that was done casually. They had to prepare their hearts to carry the holy presence of God. You see, God is a God of order, and in Scripture, when you study how the Levites prepared to minister to the Lord, all things had to be done in order. The sacrifices on the brazen altar had order. The golden candlestick and its seven lighted lamps had to be maintained and clean so the fire would never go out—just like we must maintain our hearts and keep ourselves full of the oil of the Holy Spirit so that our lights never stop burning before him. When you look at the study of the table of showbread, the bread had to be baked and prepared on a daily basis. It had to be freshly made according to the standards and the Word. This reminds me that when praise and worship leaders prepare sets, the sets must be fresh every time we put a new set together. It may be older songs we have sung a hundred times, but there must be a fresh hunger in our hearts when we step up to sing them again. We all know that if you've been in the ministry of music over a period of time, music ministry can become a routine. Our talents can take over, and we can walk through the motions, but never really connect to what's coming out of our mouths. If you get to that place, it's probably time to step down, get your heart right with God again, and find your connection with Him. We're to bring a fresh anointing whenever we step on the platform.

If you keep reading in First Chronicles 15, the preparation of David's tabernacle also involved a process of sanctification for the Levitical offices. King David called the priests and the Levites to sanctify themselves as they brought up the ark of the Lord. *Sanctify* means "to be separate, to set aside what is holy unto the Lord for holy use." You can find all of these laws in Exodus 29 and Leviticus 8. It's fascinating, because priests were to be cleansed by the blood sprinkled on the right ear and toe. We are sanctified by the blood of the Lamb. Blood is atonement for sin, and it's important for cleansing. We are cleansed by the blood of the Lamb. They sanctified themselves by bathing in water. The word of God in John Chapter 17 cleanses us of all our unrighteousness. Jesus is the lamb of

God. He is the eternal word of God. (John 1:1-3). The word cleans our hearts. The priests also anointed themselves with holy oil, which was sprinkled on the right ear, the right thumb, and the right toe, symbolic of the spirit of God (I Peter 1, 2). The priests were set aside by the blood, the word, and the spirit. We see this in the book of Revelation, Chapter 19, and in 1 John 5:8-10. There are three witnesses—the blood, the water, and the Holy Spirit.

It is no different today. Worship leaders must cleanse their hearts and their minds by pleading the blood of Jesus over their sin and repenting for things they've done. They cleanse their heart with the water of the word. They wash their minds by reading and meditating on the word, and they prepare their hands and their hearts for ministry. Don't you think it's interesting that they anoint their ear, their thumb, and their toe? I find that fascinating.

All musicians will tell you that what matters most is the ear. As a musician and instrumentalist or a vocalist, it's important to know what's in and what's out of tune. You work hard to make sure that all the instruments are tuned together for harmony and unison. So many musicians today pick up praise and worship songs by ear. That tells me it's important to pay attention to what you listen to. What are you allowing through your ear gate? What things are you listening to? Be careful what you open yourself up to spiritually when you're listening to certain songs.

The hand is vital if you're a musician. A few years back I had a car accident. I was rear-ended by someone texting on his phone. The airbags in my Toyota 4Runner exploded, and the explosion broke my right wrist. I had to go through extensive physical therapy to get my strength back so that I could play piano again. What's funny about this is that after all the therapy, my right hand ended up being stronger than my left. If you're a guitar player or keyboard player and you're right-handed, you know how important the thumb is to the rest of the hand.

Then after the hand is anointed, they anointed the foot. Well, as musicians, we always run pedals for our guitars or keyboards. The feet are important for musicians. We can inspire and lead others into the presence of God through our movements on the stage. Our feet can lead us into the presence of God or take us into places we should not be. If you're a musician, your feet can drive the drums and lead an entire congregation. A great drummer can kick the devil's head through the kick on his drum. He can literally kick darkness out of people's lives on the drum set. Again, God chose the foot to be anointed.

The bottom line for all musicians is that when we minister to the Lord in the church, it's something that we do that is holy. He looks at our hearts and our intent. He can take less skilled musicians and move through them because of the purity of their hearts: the reason we know that is because of the tabernacle of David.

The tabernacle of Moses had no music. The only sacrifices they were offered in the tabernacle of Moses were animal sacrifices. God did not want them to just offer an animal for the atonement of sin and then go on and continue to sin. What He really wanted from them was their hearts. So, when the tabernacle of David was established, King David established the sacrifice of praise. In the tabernacle of Moses, you were to enter the gates with thanksgiving in your heart to come into His courts with praise—then offer your animal sacrifice. Later, King David establishes worship on the temple mount 24 hours a day, seven days a week. He trains hundreds and hundreds of musicians to work together at all different times to minister unto the Lord. No performance mentality in the tabernacle existed. They were to minister to God, not to other men. No audiences existed to observe and clap at the wonderful performances. The only person to please was the Holy Spirit.

God is always looking for the heart.

CHAPTER 2

Priestly Function of Worship Leaders

Who may ascend into the hill of the LORD?
Or who may stand in His holy place?
He who has clean hands and a pure heart,
Who has not lifted up his soul to an idol, Nor sworn deceitfully.

Psalm 24:3-4

"Great worship leaders carry God's vision in their heart"

~Jeremy Riddle

The early church had so many tasks to accomplish just as we do to-day. Churches minister to the sick, help set people free, feed the poor, and reach out to those that are isolated and hurting. We have powerful counseling ministries and marriage seminars, we hold workshops to help those who are emotionally upset, and we have workshops to minister to those who are addicted to drugs and alcohol. We rescue abused children and take care of our elderly.

All of those are noble and important in the body of Christ. But we cannot forget that our primary purpose when we come together is to worship and glorify Christ. The main role in our churches is to come together and to sing of His greatness, to minister to Him, and to hear from the men and women of God who bring us messages inspired by the Holy Spirit. Jesus is our high priest, and as believers we are called as priests unto God. We can see this royal priesthood revealed in the ministry of Melchizedek in Psalm 110:4:

> *The LORD has sworn And will not relent, "You are a priest forever According to the order of Melchizedek."*

We also see it later in the ministry of King David, but it was ultimately fulfilled by Jesus Christ, our eternal high priest. As believers, we now operate under and through Him. Even though leading worship is a lot of fun – preparing sets, rehearsing sets, learning new worship songs – we can't lose sight of the fact that those who are called of God are separated unto the ministry by the Holy Spirit and then they are sent out to do the work of the Lord (Acts 13:2). When we step onto a platform to lead praise and worship, we are stepping into a priestly role just like the others who operate in fivefold ministry gifts.

Our service to the Lord is a valuable and important role that has its roots in the Old Testament priesthood. By looking at the requirements and history of the Levites, we can receive a clear revelation of our continual sacrifice of praise as worship leaders. The tribe of Levi was the family appointed under Aaron, Moses' brother, to be the priests for the children of Israel. They were given clear instructions about what to wear, how to worship, and how to receive offerings. This was a high-level job that was appointed by God, and there were consequences for not carrying out their assignments as the Lord had instructed. Because they represented the people before God, how they conducted their lives was very important to the Lord.

God set up a progression of how the priests were to enter into His presence in the tabernacle of Moses. They began in the outer court by washing themselves, overseeing the sacrificial offerings, and blessing the people. Only the high priest was allowed in the inner court, or the Most Holy Place. Reverence for the Most Holy Place cannot be understated. It held the Ark of the covenant and it was where the presence of God was evident. After Solomon's Temple was built and the Ark of the covenant was put into the Most Holy Place, the distinct presence of God could be seen by all the people. First Kings 8:10-11 records:

> 10 *And it came to pass, when the priests came out of the holy place, that the cloud filled the house of the LORD,*
> 11 *so that the priests could not continue ministering because of the cloud; for the glory of the LORD filled the house of the LORD.*

So how do we begin worship? We enter into the outer court with thanksgiving in our hearts in our private time with the Lord and in our corporate worship. Because we're grateful for what He's done for us, we sing songs that express our heartfelt thanks to God. We joyfully express our love to Him by spending time in His presence with music, singing, clapping, dancing and raising our hands to the Lord. We linger in the outer courts of praise as we draw closer and closer into His presence.

There was a very heavy, thick curtain that separated the holy place from the Most Holy Place. It was a six-inch rug that hung between the outer court and the inner court. Exodus 26:33 describes the veil that was hung:

> *And you shall hang the veil from the clasps. Then you shall bring the ark of the Testimony in there, behind the veil. The veil shall be a divider for you between the holy place and the Most Holy.*

This inner room is an earthly parallel of the throne room of God. When the people saw how the presence of God or the fire of God came out and consumed their offering, they were moved and fell down on their faces and shouted before God.

When Jesus died on the cross for us, that physical veil which separated the holy place from the holy of holies was supernaturally torn from the top to the bottom (Matt. 27:51). Mankind was not separated from God anymore. Because of the blood of Jesus Christ, we can now boldly enter into God's presence.

Next, we overcome our thought life and the attacks of the enemy and we choose to enter into a higher form of praise through music in our worship. We draw nearer to Him, and we are changed by His goodness. Tears of joy flow and we dance before Him as our physical expression is released. We become unaware of what is going on around us because we no longer care whether people are watching. We just want to honor Him and acknowledge Him for His goodness. Some kneel, bow, lay on the floor, or dance before Him to express their love. Without even thinking about it, we have passed from the holy place into the holy of holies. We have come into His presence.

Cleansing

The requirements for worship haven't changed. God has always required that the priests do certain tasks, and He requires them of us as well so that we can draw close to Him. One of those requirements was for the priesthood to wash their hands and feet before they ministered to the Lord.

> *19 for Aaron and his sons shall wash their hands and their feet in water from it.*
> *20 When they go into the tabernacle of meeting, or when they come near the altar to minister, to burn an offering made by fire to the LORD, they shall wash with water, lest they die.*
> *21 So they shall wash their hands and their feet, lest they die. And it shall be a statute forever to them--to him and his descendants throughout their generations."*
>
> *Exodus 30:19-21*

That should remind us every day before we step on the platform that perpetual repentance positions us to be used powerfully by the Lord when we minister to Him. Our repentant, clean hearts enable us to come boldly into God's presence. Deal with what's in your heart, ask God to forgive you, and repent of anything that hinders you from entering into His presence. God gives grace to the humble (James 4:6). When we are willing to live a life of repentance and love, God will use us in ways that will blow our minds.

God is a good God, and He loves to use people who are broken and dependent on Him. He loves to use people who seek Him with all of their hearts. Not perfect people. Not people who think they deserve something. He's looking for the people who love Him and seek Him and keep their hearts clean. Those are the servant hearts He loves to use in ministry. When you deal with your heart, your motives can be seen in your life. You will reflect that humble, broken heart as you minister to others and lead them. When you clean up your heart, it enables you to come boldly before him and help others.

God loves the brokenhearted, and He creates beauty out of their brokenness. Oftentimes difficult situations lead to the greatest promotions in the Kingdom of God. As a person learns to yield to Jesus as Lord and to obey Him, a new life begins. No longer does that person see themselves as broken, but they embrace the new life of freedom that God has for them. God loves to take people who have been through the hardest situations and put them in a place where their healed hearts can be on display for others to see. Some of the most effective praise and worship leaders I know are the ones who have gone through the most. Because God has healed them, they have a great love for Him. They have been changed by the goodness and the grace of God, and because of that transformation, they are positioned to be used by God to reflect His goodness, grace, and glory.

Cleanse your heart of all bitterness as you prepare to worship before the Lord (Heb. 12:15). Ministry can be very difficult. We can get to the point where we're so frustrated and so bitter that we don't want to have anything to do with the ministry anymore. We all love God, but dealing with God's people at times can be very difficult. People are imperfect. You've just got to love them even though they can hurt us and break our hearts sometimes. Be quick to repent of your wrong attitude or actions. You were chosen for this time in human history, you are special before

God, and your music is designed by God to honor and glorify Him. To keep yourself in the right position before God, read the Word, meditate on the Word, and obey the Word. As you do, He is cleansing you (Eph. 5:25-27).

Consecrated Life

As a priest, Aaron was appointed as the first type of praise leader, and his sons were also appointed as priests. The Aaronic priesthood was set aside and sanctified from the world; they were made holy and were completely consecrated unto the Lord.

> "Speak to Aaron, saying: 'No man of your descendants in
> succeeding generations,
> who has any defect, may approach to offer the bread of his God.
>
> Leviticus 21:17

The above Scripture is a picture or type of Jesus. Jesus is perfect and is without defect. Today we are made perfect in what Jesus did for us on the cross. As priests before God, we must do everything with reverence and honor. The ultimate goal for this priesthood was for man to draw near to God. It's so important that we as believers know and obey the instructions that we get from the Word of God. We don't come into God's presence in a careless manner. We become ineffective leaders if we choose to live in disobedience to God's principles. Aaron's two sons, Nadab and Abihu, learned a hard lesson when they dishonored God's procedures and offered a sacrifice out of order. Leviticus 10:1-3:

> Then Nadab and Abihu, the sons of Aaron, each took his censer and put fire
> in it, put incense on it, and offered profane fire before the LORD,
> which He had not commanded them.
> So fire went out from the LORD and devoured them,
> and they died before the LORD.
> And Moses said to Aaron, "This is what the LORD spoke, saying: 'By those

who come near Me I must be regarded as holy; And before all the people I must be glorified.' " So Aaron held his peace.

These two men had been properly trained and ordained as priests, but they still tried to perform their duties their way. As a result, they were consumed by fire! Be careful. Judge yourself lest you be judged. God has chosen you for this time in human history to worship and glorify him, but He expects you to do it with character and integrity. Hebrews 12:14 tells us to "pursue peace with all people, and holiness, without which no one will see the Lord..." No one is perfect. I am far from it. But I also know that I have to run after holiness. It's not something that automatically happens just because we're born again. We have to want it.

God has enabled me and called me to teach and train the next generation of worship leaders alive today, and I take this calling very seriously. You've got to know your calling so you can walk it out with as much integrity as possible. As Peter said, "You are a chosen generation, a royal priesthood, a holy nation, His own special people" (1 Peter 2:9). Remind yourself that what you're doing is holy. God desires that we would walk as His children. And because of what Jesus did on the cross, we can now share in Christ's ministry through his blood. According to Scripture, I am walking in the New Testament priesthood, and my life is to be a light for the lost and the dying. The apostle Paul urged all of us to live a life worthy of our calling. Find out what measures up to God's standard for instruction and praise, and guard the worship service so that the music and the customs of this world don't enter in.

Being a priest unto God may not sound all that exciting in today's world, but it is a responsibility to uphold God's order. It is what we do for the Lord and how we minister to Him that truly gives Him honor and glory. We see this later on in the life of King David who was not only a king, but he also functioned as a priest. King David set up the tabernacle and brought up the Ark to the Mount in Jerusalem. This typified the coming priestly ministry of Jesus Christ. As we come to God, God comes near to us (James 4:8). Because of Jesus laying down his life on the cross, now we have a better covenant and we can enter boldly into God's presence.

We are now able to draw near to God in our praise and worship. Yes, we are operating under a covenant of grace, but we are never to take for granted the holiness of what we are doing or the sacredness of what we are offering unto God.

Priest's Clothing

Priests would prepare themselves to minister to the Lord by wearing distinctive clothing that was different from all other men's clothing. They were given clear instructions as to what they were to wear at all times. The garments were a reflection of their relationship with God. They wore linen breeches, and one coat of one piece of fabric. In addition, they wore a four-colored girdle and a linen covering. Linen always represents righteousness in the Bible, and we are now the righteousness of God in Christ Jesus.

> *10 And the priest shall put on his linen garment, and his linen trousers he shall put on his body, and take up the ashes of the burnt offering which the fire has consumed on the altar, and he shall put them beside the altar. 11 Then he shall take off his garments, put on other garments, and carry the ashes outside the camp to a clean place.*
>
> *Leviticus 6:10-11*

Just like the Levitical priests had to change their garments, we should purify our hearts as we minister to Him. Moses commanded his people to sanctify themselves or to wash their clothes (Exo. 19:10). This would've been quite a feat during Bible times without the modern inventions of washers and dryers. How they were able to keep clean in an era where they didn't have the ability to wash or cleanse their garments is interesting.

Before you step on that platform to lead worship, it is important that you judge yourself and cleanse yourself by repenting of anything that could hinder your praise and worship before the people. It's so important that we judge ourselves lest we be judged. I always tell my students, "Don't worry about dealing with everybody else's sin; just deal with your sin first." Do everything you can to pull that plank out of your eye before you try to turn around and pull a plank out of somebody else's. God will honor you and He will honor your heart.

After the priesthood cleansed themselves and dressed accordingly, they would be anointed with oil. Oil is a symbol of the Holy Spirit. Today believers are priests who have the anointing of the Holy Spirit abiding within them when they receive Jesus as their Lord and Savior.

Maintaining Fire on the Altar

Maintaining the fires in the temple was a full-time job for the priest. He had to feed the fire and clean up the ashes. Priest had busy lives and they had to work hard to keep the fires burning on the altars of sacrifice, and that wasn't an easy job. Fires have to be perpetually fueled so that the bottom of the fire will not go out.

> 9 *"Command Aaron and his sons, saying, 'This is the law of the burnt offering: The burnt offering shall be on the hearth upon the altar all night until morning, and the fire of the altar shall be kept burning on it.*
> 12 *And the fire on the altar shall be kept burning on it; it shall not be put out. And the priest shall burn wood on it every morning, and lay the burnt offering in order on it; and he shall burn on it the fat of the peace offerings.*
> 13 *A fire shall always be burning on the altar; it shall never go out.*
>
> *Leviticus 6:9, 12-13*

As believers and as worship leaders, we must fuel our love for the Lord through prayer and fasting. We must fuel our spirits so that when we lead worship, the fire of our relationship can be seen by the congregation. Paul told Timothy that we had to fan the fire within us (2 Timothy 1:6). Ministering to the Lord and to others is never ending. It is part of the minister's lifestyle.

In the same way, maintaining or taking care of their own "temple" is something that praise and worship leaders have to do when they minister in the local church. Leading praise and worship can become habitual and even boring. However, you can't take for granted what you have been called by God to do. If we allow ashes to accumulate – thinking about how spectacular the last service was – then the fresh fire cannot burn. We have to move forward with what the spirit is telling us to do today. Dwelling on what God has done in the past will stunt your worship today. Fresh fire needs fresh fuel, and we must perpetually fuel or fan the flame within us.

Offer Sacrifices

One of the most important roles of the priesthood was to offer sacrifices. Once a year the high priest would enter into the holy of holies (or a place called "Most Holy") and would offer sacrifices to God on behalf of the people to atone for their sins. A sacrifice is costly. It is always worth more than the person can easily afford. It is holy before the Lord, and it is not easy or convenient.

Our sacrifice of praise is what we sing to Him. We offer Him our hearts through our words and music. As worship leaders, our job is to help the people to offer those sacrifices unto God. We enable them to glorify God and to honor God with our ministry of music. There is nothing in the world like an on-fire praise and worship service where the presence of God falls as the people offer a sacrifice of praise. It's truly a holy thing.

> *Therefore by Him let us continually offer the sacrifice of praise to God, that is, the fruit of our lips, giving thanks to His name.*
>
> *Hebrews 13:15*

Worship leaders have to ask themselves, "Am I leading praise and worship the way God would have me do it? Are we offering acceptable worship to Him? Or are we bringing the world and our idols into the house of God?"

Aaronic priests were to enter daily into the tabernacle, and today's worship leaders daily present music for our local churches.

Don't ever look back on your life and regret difficulty you've been through. That difficulty will often position you to be used by Him. Because of what Jesus did on the cross for us, He has now made us clean. We can take our broken-heartedness and heaviness and use that as a sacrifice to give Him honor and glory. He will give us beauty for ashes, and He will take our mourning and turn it into joy (Isa. 61:3). As a priest before God, bring him your thanksgiving and praise. Bring your offerings to Him through your music, your money, and your life. Present your body as a living sacrifice to Him.

A priest also blessed the people and their sacrifices that were brought to the temple (Lev. 9:22-24). As ministers before the Lord, we similarly bless the people by giving them an opportunity to worship the Lord with holy music and lyrics. A priest would have also been transformed as he witnessed the dedication of the people and their dependence on Jehovah as they presented animals for sacrifice that would ultimately wash them clean. The ministers of music see the people's faces in worship, and with holy hands lifted and mouths filled with praise, the burdens they brought in are left on the altar for both the minister and the people.

Worship in My Day

I was raised in a church where the congregation sang from a hymnal with music that was somber. We felt awkward raising our hands or demonstrating our love for God. I couldn't relate to the music or worship, nor did I understand it. I'm thankful that I was allowed by God to bring freedom to a generation of worship leaders who could study the Word of God and glean revelation from it while singing and praising God in a way that would reach this generation. I tried to fully teach and train my students to love God biblically and scripturally while using new styles and ways of ministering praise and worship to the next generation. I've seen God move in glorious ways as His presence filled my classroom many times through our praise and worship sets. We were able to minister unto Him and to bless Him, and He gets all honor and glory. Our lives and our music are an offering unto him. The music that we create, play, and sing to Him is how we honor Him with our talents and abilities. As we do this, we are sanctified by God. Just as He used the priests of old to minister before Him, He takes our gifts and creativity to minister to others.

CHAPTER 3

Old Testament Patterns of Worship

> *"Before there was a Tabernacle of David in the city of David*
> *there was a Tabernacle in the heart of King David"*
> *~Rick Pino*

We can learn a lot about today's worship by the way God set it up in biblical times. He detailed how, why and when the Israelites were to worship. He was specific about the organization and the administration of worship, which is the pattern and structure for us today. The Old Testament pattern for worship is important because it reveals what pleases the Lord and what worship was intended for. It's a great joy to study these principles or patterns so that you can understand how they relate to New Testament worship.

One of the most important biblical laws of interpretation is called the law of much mention. Basically, it tells you to pay attention to how much a topic is covered in Scripture. Tabernacles are covered extensively in the Old Testament. These were the places where God and His people would meet. It's where they entered into His presence. Because our job is to usher people into the presence of God, every worship leader should understand the history of tabernacles and why God chose each of them as a way to meet with the people.

There were several tabernacles mentioned in the Old Testament, and they all symbolically point to Jesus Christ. An in-depth look into each of these tabernacles will show New Testament worship leaders some areas where the Church can rediscover why certain worship requirements are in place.

Tabernacle of Moses

After the children of Israel were delivered out of Egypt and were under Moses' direction in the desert, they were given instructions to build a tent structure in the middle of their camp where the people could learn to worship Jehovah. The children of Israel had been in slavery in Egypt for 400 years. They did not know the God of Abraham, Isaac, and Jacob (Israel). This was all new to them. Being delivered from captivity was a miracle, but it was through the Tabernacle of Moses that they would be reintroduced to the God who brought about their freedom.

The Tabernacle of Moses was a pattern or blueprint that was given in exact detail by God. The dimensions, furniture, and fabrics were meticulously recorded in Scripture. This tabernacle was a portable tent that could be set up in each new campsite as the children of Israel moved throughout the holy land. It was a place where people would go to worship, and it was a temporary dwelling place that housed the Ark of the Covenant. The Levitical priests were in charge of the tabernacle and maintained the tent and all its furnishings.

Entering the tabernacle is exciting. It's called the Gates of Praise. We are to come into God's presence with thanksgiving in our hearts and enter His courts with praise. The entrance was guarded by the priests who would assist the Israelites bringing their sacrifices to the tabernacle. Everyone who needed atonement for sin had to bring an offering and then it would be sacrificed for by the priests according to God's instructions given to Moses.

Whenever I enter into praise and worship, one of the first things I do is repent of my sin. I know I can go into God's presence immediately because of what He did on the cross, but I think getting my heart right with God and repenting of things I may or may not have done is important. It's the process I naturally go through when I am preparing my heart to worship God. I don't want to have anything in my life that could hinder what He is doing or saying to me. I love making sure I am right with Him at all times.

Offering a sacrifice of praise is biblical as we see this in the first station of the tabernacle, the Bronze Altar, which was built for sacrifice and atonement. The Levitical priesthood sacrificed animals that the people brought to them for the atonement, or forgiveness, of sin. This was a messy, smelly place. The animals were tied to the horns on the altar, the throat was slit, and the blood was poured out. It was ugly and brutal. But our sin is ugly and brutal as well, and that's why the blood of Jesus Christ is so precious. This is why as praise and worship leaders we should never tire of singing songs about the blood of Jesus. I remember R.W. Schambach, a very well-known healing evangelist, speaking at my church, and when he went to lay hands on the sick, he wanted the worship team to sing about the Blood of Jesus. Why? When we corporately sing about the Blood of Jesus, the power of God manifests and people are healed! The Blood never loses its power.

After you get things right with God, is time to get cleaned up. The priests would go to the next station, the water laver. It was a large bronze bowl filled with water and the priests would clean up after the sacrifice. The water in the bowl reflected the image of the priest's face back to him and reminded him when they were cleaning up that they needed to be made clean. We always see ourselves and our sin when we are reading the Word of God. The Word reflects back to us what adjustments we must make and how we must align our hearts with Christ. I love reading the Word of God and allowing it to work on me. That's why we should be singing scripture in our worship services. When we are writing or singing worship in our churches, don't settle for entertaining music that is shallow and has very little substance scripturally. Stick to the Word of God. What God has spoken in scripture, He wants it sung back to Him. When we honor God and His Word, His spirit falls and then the captives are set free. Once we get into God's presence through sacrifice and repentance, it's time to worship.

Worship happens at the table of showbread. I am reminded of the bread that we break when we take communion at the table of showbread. The bread had to always be fresh and it was symbolic of fellowship. When we come together with other believers and we break bread together or we eat a meal together, we are in fellowship with each other. That's what happens at this point. We are now in God's presence and we share with Him. As worship leaders it's important to remember that we must always bring a fresh meal or a fresh set when it's time to lead. It's easy to get stuck in a rut and sing what works and what is comfortable, but we will see God move when we sing what He wants when He wants it. It's kind of like going out to dinner and having a really good meal. It's just satisfying. When we sing fresh worship music, we feel full and satisfied in His presence.

Next was the candlestick, a large solid gold menorah made to look like pomegranate branches and flowers. The Bible says we are to bear spiritual fruit and it should all be lit by the fire of God. The seven lights of the candlestick were symbolic for the seven spirits of God. We see references to this in the visions of the throne room in Revelations 4. The lamps light our way. We are illuminated by God's presence and His spirit. He enables us to hear and to be enlightened by the Holy Spirit.

The priests always worked in the candlelight. The lights had to be cleaned and filled with fresh oil. The wicks had to be cleaned away and the oil bowls filled. When we clean up ourselves, we make sure our oil or the presence of the Holy Spirit is fresh and full. Then God's spirit comes to illuminate us and our spirit. He shows us what to do. We produce spiritual fruit and His holy spirit shows us what to do and where to go. Churches today get so much pressure to make the church service short that we miss the opportunity to really dwell in His presence. Trust me, when the Holy Spirit is moving, no one wants to go home. No one wants to leave. The Holy Spirit and the gifts of the spirit make this walk with Jesus Christ FUN and exciting. When God's spirit is moving, no one is in a hurry.

The priests attended to the altar of incense morning and evening. It was very holy. Nadab and Abihu were both struck dead when lightning came out from that altar after they offered improperly prepared incense (Lev. 10:1-3). God is a holy God and we don't get to do things our way or do things that don't line up with his heart or with his spirit. God's ways of being worshipped must be honored. When we do. the prayers of the saints rise up to heaven and He hears our prayer. As worship leaders, we sing our prayers and we pray our songs. What we sing is an extension of our prayer life. When we sing from our heart, it is a beautiful smelling aroma to God. His presence comes. We also know in scripture that when the Glory of God falls or the Shekinah glory of God falls, it looks like a cloud or a mist. I don't mind modern day fog machines in church. They make me cough a lot on stage and I know they make the sanctuary look great with the lighting, but I love it when His presence and glory are so tangible that we don't need man-modified glory clouds.

Finally, it's time to go into the holiest place of all where the Ark of the Covenant dwells – the Holy of Holies. By going through all of the stations, the high priest was prepared to enter this holy place. He had to go in it with his heart right before God because if he didn't, he would be struck dead. They would tie a rope around the high priest's ankle in case he fell over dead while he was behind the veil in the Holy of Holies. No one wanted to go into the Holy of Holies and pull out a dead high priest. The Levitical priests would carry the Ark of the Lord on their shoulders as they would move from one campsite to the next.

The mercy seat was between the wings of the two cherubim sitting on the ark. This is the place where his manifest presence would dwell. Aren't you thankful for mercy? Aren't you thankful we serve a holy God and we can come into His presence and not be afraid of judgment? The key is always walking before the lord with awe and respect. If we as worship leaders will always judge our hearts, then He doesn't have to judge us. We are free to love and worship Him. He is such a good God and it's an honor to serve Him and the people of God on a daily basis.

It is interesting that there was no music in the Tabernacle of Moses.

Tabernacle of David

The Tabernacle of David was about different from the Tabernacle of Moses. Basically, it was a tent with the ark in it on the temple mount. The priests would enter the gates with thanksgiving in their hearts. They would enter his courts with praise because the Ark of God was in full view. There was no holy of holies or veil. The sacrifice offered was a sacrifice of praise 24 hours a day, seven days a week, by sanctified and set-aside musicians whose only role was to minister to the Lord with music. This specific window of time only lasted for 40 years until Solomon's temple was built. All of the stations stayed in the tabernacle of Moses, and on the temple mount there was a tent and the ark. The stations would all return once the temple of Solomon was built and the Ark of the Covenant was transferred into the temple and then animal sacrifices would resume.

The Ark of the covenant was present in the Tabernacle of David, but there was no veil separating the priests from God's presence. This has prophetic significance and points to the coming Messiah whose death on the cross caused the veil to be rent in two. It was in this tabernacle that David offered the sacrifice of praise. The focus was no longer on the sacrifice of animals but in offering God a musical sacrifice. Musicians were trained musically and spiritually for many months to present music before the Lord. We must do the same today.

David was a man after God's own heart. He had been anointed by the prophet and was responsible for recording the book of Psalms and organizing all of the musical instruments in the tabernacle. God was interested in the sacrifice of praise. He wanted people's hearts. He didn't want them offering an animal and going on and continuing in their sin. He wanted them to worship Him, love Him and to do what was right.

The problem with King David was that he was a man of war. He had killed thousands. God had given him supernatural ability to fight for God and for his kingdom. David was a man's man, but he was also a man who was broken before God. He knew where his strength came from. It came from the presence of God.

David was also an outstanding administrator. He was given the plans to build the temple of God, but this temple was so holy that he would not be allowed to build it. He had blood on his hands from the battles he fought. The building of the temple would pass on to his son Solomon (I Chron. 28:3).

King David was responsible for the invention of many of the musical instruments such as harps and wind, percussion (cymbals and drums), and stringed instruments that we play today. His creativity came from his desire to minister to the Lord. He was a passionate worshiper who wanted to bless the Lord.

He also understood the importance of unity among the priests. The priests were sanctified and set aside for purpose. They understood the holiness of what they were doing for God. The Levites worked fervently all year to perfect their music for their season of service before the Lord, and the role of the vocalist was incredibly important. The singer was God's human musical instrument that would release a sound from within his body. And the sound that the vocalists make would be enhanced later by harmony.

King David understood that he was responsible to highly esteem what God honored. When the ark came to Zion and it was placed in a tent, passionate worship followed. The Levites were appointed to minister before the ark of the Lord "to commemorate, to thank, and to praise the LORD God of Israel:" (1 Chronicles 16:4). The Levites knew what their roles were and they did it with all of their heart. There was creativity and passion. You see, God has no problem with loud, passionate, or dramatic worship. What He has a problem with are leaders whose hearts are not right with Him and they're leading worship to promote themselves. What they are doing is not a gift or a sacrifice. It is self-exalting, and God opposes that. It's got to be about worshipping Him, not drawing attention to ourselves.

They would passionately worship God until the glory filled the temple. This glory came in the form of a cloud that could be seen.

> [13] *indeed it came to pass, when the trumpeters and singers were as one, to make one sound to be heard in praising and thanking the LORD, and when they lifted up their voice with the trumpets and cymbals and instruments of music, and praised the LORD, saying: "For He is good, For His mercy endures forever," that the house, the house of the LORD, was filled with a cloud,* [14] *so that the priests could not continue ministering because of the cloud; for the glory of the LORD filled the house of God.*
>
> 2 Chronicles 5:13-14

The greatest compliment that God can ever give a musician is His presence. Not the applause of man. Not the latest record contract. Nor the people that will to come to hear worship leaders play on a Sunday morning. No, the greatest compliment God can ever give a musician is when He graces that service with His presence. When the glory of God comes, that's when people's hearts can be changed. That's when real lives are touched. If you've never experienced anything like this, when it happens, it will mark you forever. Once you feel the presence of God on you as you sing, nothing else in the world will satisfy. No drug or alcohol can satisfy you more than the presence of God. The anointing becomes addictive.

The Ark of the Covenant sat in this tabernacle of David for four years. This is our modern-day pattern that we follow corporately and individually. It's referred to in Acts 15:16-17:

> [16] *'After this I will return And will rebuild the tabernacle of David, which has fallen down; I will rebuild its ruins, And I will set it up;* [17] *So that the rest of mankind may seek the LORD, Even all the Gentiles who are called by My name, Says the LORD who does all these things.'*

This also refers to the end time millennial reign of Christ. It would be the end of animal sacrifices. You can see references to this in the Old Testament as well in the Book of Amos:

"On that day I will raise up The tabernacle of David, which has fallen down, And repair its damages; I will raise up its ruins, And rebuild it as in the days of old;

Amos 9:11

Today's worship is a fulfillment of prophecy from Acts and Amos. It incorporates all that the Tabernacle of David represented: passionate worship, singing, musical instruments, and the presence of God coming down in a glory cloud on the worship service. Are we allowing these into our services? Are we giving honor to the One who is to be worshipped more than the gift of music that we possess? We can recreate this worship as we honor what God honors, staying humble with our talents, and using them for His purposes.

Solomon's Temple

Solomon's temple was magnificent. It was much like the tabernacle of Moses, yet it was permanent and glorious. The floors and walls were covered with gold and precious jewels. Everything that was built in the temple was symbolic of God's goodness and his glory. After the Ark was put into the holy of holies, the bars that were used to move the Ark were pulled out because the Ark had a permanent dwelling place. There were two Angels covering the place where the Ark sat. When atonement was offered for the entire nation of Israel once a year, the priests would enter the holy of holies to perform their priestly duties.

Over the years, however, this temple began to fall apart. When Israel was defeated by foreign kings, Jerusalem and the temple were invaded, and the gold was stripped from the walls and the floor. At one time, this temple was misused with altars that were built to false gods and sodomite activities that took place there. Animals were even stabled in this inner court. This temple was completely destroyed by the Chaldeans who took everything of value to Babylon. Then they burned this temple to the ground.

When I went to Israel in 2001, we took the underground tour of the temple. I could not help noticing how beautifully the temple was built.

The large bricks were the size of a classroom chalkboard. The only way that this temple could've been destroyed was to set it on fire. It was built of limestone, and logs were set around it and then set on fire. The limestone exploded in the temple was destroyed.

Herod's Temple

When King Herod gained control of Judah, he rebuilt the temple. It wasn't as grand as Solomon's, but it was larger. Herod didn't build it because he had a heart for God; he was just passionate about constructing buildings. The temple lacked some of the furniture in Solomon's Temple, and the Ark of the Lord was also gone.

Herod's Temple was really set up to appease the Jewish people. And it was in Herod's Temple that Jesus ministered. This is also the temple where Jesus overturned the tables of the moneychangers (Matt. 21:12-13). Jesus was not happy with how worship had become marketed and merchandised by the Jewish leaders. These leaders were taking advantage of the Jewish people by ripping them off financially, and Jesus was grieved.

Jesus was always dealing with the heart of man. He was always looking at the motive of men's hearts. Jesus prophesied that the temple would be destroyed one day and "not one brick would remain on another" in this temple (Matt. 24:2). In 70 A.D., that prophecy came to pass. The temple and the surrounding buildings were completely destroyed, and the gold was melted and the stones were removed, thus fulfilling Jesus' prophecy.

Times of Worship

Understanding why they worshipped in the Old Testament gives us insight into why we worship today. In many instances, worship preceded victory. Imagine putting praisers out in front of an army as they did in Second Chronicles 20. As worship leaders, we can learn from those who have gone before us and have used worship in various circumstances.

King Jehoshaphat saw music as an integral part when it came to inspiring his army. As a result, the whole army of God rose to face the enemy in a positive manner (2 Chron. 20). King David worked with his army commanders to set apart musicians and singers, and he set aside others for temple service of prophesying with musical instruments. They were to wait, study, and practice their ministry so they could function effectively under the anointing.

Hezekiah worked closely with the Levites in the temple of God. He brought in the singers and the prophets, and he gave orders that the sacrifice or the burnt offering was to be put on the altar. When the sacrifice was offered, the people bowed down and worshipped while the singers and the trumpeters played. Consequently, the service of the temple was reestablished. And the people rejoiced:

So all the assembly worshiped, the singers sang, and the trumpeters sounded; all this continued until the burnt offering was finished.
And when they had finished offering, the king and all who were present with him bowed and worshiped.

2 Chronicles 29:28-29

The Book of Ezra is an interesting study about worship. The Israelites had been in Babylonian captivity and were miraculously given permission by the King of Persia, Cyrus, to begin building their temple back in Jerusalem. As the foundation of the temple was laid, the priests were in their robes and in place to praise the Lord; their ministry created an emotional response in the atmosphere. The older men wept and shouted for joy because they knew the glory of God and saw that it was back in the house. God's presence had come back. When the Holy Spirit moves, it's not emotionalism. When you've known the presence of God and then you tangibly feel it once again, it's a very emotional experience. The joy of seeing the temple's foundation laid was so exhilarating that the people's shouting was heard from far away (Ezra 3:13). This signified the return of the Jews to their land, and it was a reason to rejoice.

At the dedication of the temple, Nehemiah brought worshipers together into large choirs. They went in opposite directions up to the top of the wall and took their place in the house of God (Neh. 12:27-43). As a choir director, this portion of Scripture makes me happy. I can imagine these two choirs echoing off each other, worshiping God. It was the beginning of Dolby sound, or sounds coming from two different locations. It also reminds me of call and response music that operates in the hearts of believers. The music and singing were very important in dedicating the temple as the people sang and worshipped together in unity.

Now we know that those who don't know God can use music for idolatry and idol worship. King Nebuchadnezzar of Babylon demanded worship: "…at the time you hear the sound of the horn, flute, harp, lyre, and psaltery, in symphony with all kinds of music, you shall fall down and worship the gold image that King Nebuchadnezzar has set up" (Daniel 3:5). It has happened in the past and could happen again. The time is coming when God is going to deal with those that play with worship. God did it then and He will do it again. He is not going to turn his back on those who are using things that are supposed to be holy in an unholy way. He is a holy God. Jesus came to fulfill the Old Testament, not to abolish it.

Worship Today

In the Old Testament, the temple building was made of stone and cedar. The presence of God would fall in places made my human hands. The Tabernacles were made of all kinds of different substances: cedar wood, animal skins, linen, bronze, gold, shittim wood. But we are the modern temple. Now we are the temple of the Holy Spirit, and because our temple is flesh, it would mean that God would use us in a greater degree. God dwells in the praises of his people. If you want to know where God is, just listen to the body of Christ singing. I have no problem with loud worship, but in today's modern worship services when the band pulls out and you hear the bride of Christ singing in one accord, that's where God is.

Those Old Testament principles of consecration are still important today. If you are called to be a minister of music, then you are going to live a life of a minister. That means ministry comes before music. You have an anointing from God to open heaven and set captives free. Allow the gift of God to be used for the kingdom of God. It's not about trying to get rich and famous or sign a record deal; it's about blessing the Lord.

Ultimately God looks at your heart. He knows if your heart is to minister to him. My heart in this day and hour is to see musicians and singers fulfill the destiny that God has on their life. I'm excited about all the new technology that we have to reach the lost. But we can never forget that we are first and foremost called to minister to the Lord. We are called to prophesy light into darkness. We are called to set captives free. We are called to invite the presence of God into services. We don't worship idols. We don't bring idolatry into the house of God. We don't lift up ourselves, nor do we seek the idolatry of fame.

Right now, with all of the reality TV and all of the availability of YouTube, it would be very easy to seek fame instead of to seek God. It would be very easy to see ourselves promoted instead of promoting the kingdom of heaven. I'm not against making money. In fact, I know ministers of music must have money in order to survive. Trust me; I understand that better than anyone else. Yes, you should make money off the things that you create. Just be careful with how you market the anointing so that you're not writing and creating music that's going to make a buck instead of glorify God.

My students over the years can tell you that the most important moments in my classroom were not the days that we were preparing for contest. My students always had to sing classical choral music in order for us to compete at state contests. There was a purpose for all of that. The classical choral *a cappella* music trains vocalists to harmonize. The only way to learn to sing harmony is to sing with other vocalists and to do it with music that's well written. Good music enables the vocalist to hear the other vocal parts as well. They didn't always enjoy it, but it did teach them an important skill set for ministry.

No, the most important moments in my classroom were the moments where we worshiped and praised the Lord. They were moments in my classroom where we glorified God and his holiness. We prayed for the student body as the Levitical priests should do. We prayed for the students to have an encounter with Christ. We prayed that Christ would move and touch the lives of the hurting and the broken. Not everything we did musically was ministry. But the music that we studied was designed on purpose to help them become skillful Levitical musicians.

God wants to restore praise and worship, and He has done a lot in the last 30 years. When I started training praise and worship leaders at my Christian school, there was no such thing as student-led praise and worship. But I had a pastor who had a heart for kids and built a Christian school so the kids could worship and honor God. He built the school where God could be glorified. He had vision for upcoming generations. This generation would worship God and honor God from a pure heart and with the right motive. These young people would lead by example in the last days. They would use all the modern technology available to them to reach the lost, but they would respect the holiness and the sacredness of God and His Word. They would do things according the biblical mandate and order. Students would honor God by singing songs that were theologically correct. They would not offer worship that pointed to a man but pointed to God. Young men and women would select songs that would enhance the believer's confession.

I'm thankful for the students that I have raised up as worshippers. And I believe with all of my heart that they want to do it the right way. They want to honor God with all of the creativity and technology that is available to them so they can reach their generation.

My concern isn't for those that I have mentored, but it's for those who haven't been taught biblically and scripturally about praise and worship. These potential worship leaders haven't had the opportunity to sit in a classroom and be taught the Word of God. They may not understand the pattern in the Old Testament and how it was fulfilled in the New Testament. Because they don't know any better, they treat church like it's just another gig or concert. I believe the Holy Spirit will honor them and their heart if they will humbly cry out to Him.

When you study the biblical patterns for worship and you do it His way with a humble heart, God will move and will bless your church with his tangible presence. I believe that understanding can birth the next great revival on the earth. Our heavenly Father longs to be worshiped. He longs to be glorified. He longs to be seen. He is our all in all. Come quickly, Lord Jesus!

When I was a kid, and God was talking to me about music, I was like, 'Okay, I'll sing mainstream music,' because I was afraid to sing Christian music to alienate my friends. Honestly, it was going on 'Idol,' having that kind of exposure, that I realized there's something different about me. I just crave God being a part of every moment.

~Lauren Daigle

CHAPTER 4

The Instruments

"Let everything that hath breath praise the LORD. Praise ye the LORD."
~Psalms 150:6

M usic is the universal language of the soul, and humans have always found new and creative ways to worship the Lord. Some
instruments are for melody or to help the worshiper sing the
melody, while others provide harmony. The rhythmic instruments keep
the beat going. It helps the worship stay structured even during an acapella
vocal sections. The rhythmic section is the backbone of any worship band
today. Everything revolves around a drummer and bass player who can
keep the band together and the tempos correct.

In modern worship, melodic instruments provide the key that the prophetic song will flow in. Staying in a key with basic chord structure is the
key to releasing the prophetic song, especially if the band is going to follow
the vocalist. We live in an exciting digital age where we can create all kinds
of sounds to release the presence of God, and I know there will be new
ones invented in the future.

The book of Psalms talks extensively about instruments. We don't
know for sure what these instruments were made of or how they were
made, but we can get a good idea from ancient coins and pottery and ar-
cheology. Our local Jewish community brought in an amazing group

called Savae that was organized by a musicologist who had studied musical instruments on ancient coins and pottery. Moshe Gorali was the founder and director of the Haifa Museum of Music, and he first started this study years ago. Since 1971, he and his team of musicologists have been working to recreate these instruments.

The study of these instruments came from linguistic- exegesis of biblical and Talmudic passages and the Mishnah (Jewish commentary). The archeological digs reveal mostly simple and unsophisticated instruments. They found rattles, cymbals, bells and flutes made of metal, earthenware or bone. Ancient coins, mosaics and engravings show these instruments were played by the people.

Researchers have learned a lot from modern Bedouins living in the Negev whose musical instruments and traditions are well known my musicologists today. These researchers have also consulted immigrants from Israel and Ethiopia. These communities and traditions have helped bring understanding to the study. Archaeological digs have confirmed that human beings were much smaller at about 1.5 meters or 4'11" in height. From those estimates of height, the researchers have been able to determine the size of their instruments.

The most difficult instruments to reproduce is the strings. Strings came mostly from animal intestines. The main concern is how they would have maintained string tension so that the strings could be tuned. Tuning has always been a musician's challenge. I know how hard it is to tune instruments today, which is why I love my digital tuner on my phone. They would have had nothing like that. In fact, I wonder how they tuned them at all. The other question centers around the sound box and some sort of bridge to hold the strings. These biblical musicians had to be determined and creative.

The most fascinating part for me was realizing how hard it would have been for these musicians to play melodies. Today in our modern culture, we always think about melody and harmony, but most of these musical instruments were percussive and shrill. They had several styles of shakers and things with bells, but the only real melodic instruments would have come from "U" shaped instruments with strings attached at the bottom and then wound up to the top bar.

Modern Worship Instruments

The acoustic guitar is the most personal sounding of all musical instruments. The keyboard, however, can sound like any instrument. Worship used to be driven by the keyboard, but that is changing now. Today they are adding pads and some melodic things in worship. The person writing the worship songs determines how the instruments are used.

We don't use a lot of strings today except in our digital keyboards that can replicate those sounds. It's very rare to have a string player. Cellos are very popular right now and have been used a lot.

Wind instruments are not used in worship too often today, but a nice pad sounds a little like good woodwinds. Most of these instruments are used in concert bands and orchestras today and usually not in the modern church. It's also a budget issue. Most churches don't have the money to pay these extra musicians.

One instrument that is still vital today is the drum. If the drummer is off, everybody is off. The drummer gives the structure for the entire worship experience. Tempos have to be correct.

Musical Instruments Designed by King David

Musical instruments in the tabernacle of David were very primitive compared to what we play today. Nonetheless, they were developed by King David, and the Levites changed music forever. A psaltery was an ancient stringed instrument similar to a lyre. It has a sounding board with the strings stretched over it. A lyre is an ancient stringed instrument consisting of a resonating tortoise shell and a crossbar that was attached by two arms and a small piece of wood.

I highly recommend you take time to study the tabernacle of David by Kevin Connor. This extensive study on the instruments in David's Tabernacle will show you just how creative King David was. Not only did he invent many of these musical instruments, but he had scribes set aside to record what these musicians sang and played. These musicians organized the book of Psalms.

Instruments of Music in Old Testament

We know from modern monuments in Egypt and Assyria and other Middle Eastern nations that musical instruments were a part of ancient culture. We worship with the same three groups of instruments today. Wind, strings and percussion – our modern guitars, keyboards and drums.

Music is all throughout the Old Testament, and it's interesting to study the language in the scriptures and see how these instruments were practically used. The music of Israel was glorifying to God. Worship and praise were always part of Jewish culture. Worship was embraced by the Jewish people. These terms show us that there were 28 instruments: percussion, wind, string and the ultimate instrument – the human voice. We know from research there were musical terms used that described mood and how the new words were sung to old tunes. Josephus is a reliable source, and scholars look to him to understand ancient music.

The Shofar

I have always enjoyed studying the shofar. The shofar signifies everything that is dear to God, and it's a blessing to study this instrument. The shofar is a ram's horn, and it was one of the first instruments to be played by the Jewish people. I was first introduced to this instrument when I was directing the Tabernacle of Moses production at our Christian school. Honestly, the instrument looks rather strange. It is a long, stretched-out horn that is kind of smelly on the inside, but when someone can play it well, you know in your spirit that it is a special sound.

The shofar is a divine instrument that is mentioned often in scripture. In biblical times, there were no such things as microphones and speakers. Biblical leaders had no way of communicating with Israelites, and so a system of communication was developed through a primitive horn. By blowing into this ram's horn, the priests were able to signal things to the surrounding community. This instrument is so important that it's deserving of our time and study in this book. It symbolizes the voice of the prophet (Ezekiel 33:1-8).

SHOFAR' (a Hebrew word which according to Strong's Dictionary, #07782, is translated *'trumpet'* in 68 of the 72 times it appears in the Old Testament). The trumpet is important because it was blown as a sign of victory. When we blow the shofar today, it's symbolic of our call for divine help or assistance. We know that sound releases the spirit realm to move. That's why it's such a joy to hear someone blow a shofar who really knows how to do it. There are so many Bible references to study about the trumpet, but before we get into that, here are some quotes from the Jewish Encyclopedia:

> "It was the voice of the shofar 'exceeding loud' issuing from the thick cloud on Sinai that made all in the camp tremble (Ex xix. 16, xx.18): and for this reason while other musical instruments were in each age constructed according to the most advanced contemporary practice, the trumpet family being represented by the long straight silver 'hazozerah,' ...the shofar has never varied in structure from its prehistoric simplicity and crudity.
>
> ...The curved shofar is symbolic of the contrite heart repenting on the most solemn days of Rosh ha Shanah and Yom Kippur.
>
> The shofar represents the windpipe, the spiritual part of the body alongside the gullet, through which the food or the earthly part passes. The sound of the shofar awakens the Higher Mercy = 'Rahamim'... The object of the second and third series of 'teki-ot' is to bewilder and stagger Satan, who, at first imagining that the Jews are merely complying with the Law, is surprised by the second blowing, thinking perhaps that the Messiah is coming, and finally is dumbfounded, expecting the Resurrection, with which his power will finally cease."[1]

---

[1] 2006-2011 Jewish Encyclopedia.com.

Let's look at some biblical references to the shofar to see when it was blown:

- Shofars were blown at Mount Sinai.

Ex. 19:16
And it came to pass on the third day in the morning, that there were thunders and lightnings, and a thick cloud upon the mount, and the voice of the trumpet exceeding loud; so that all the people that was in the camp trembled.

Ex. 19:19
And when the voice of the trumpet sounded long, and waxed louder and louder, Moses spake, and God answered him by a voice.

Ex. 20:18
And all the people saw the thunderings, and the lightnings, and the noise of the trumpet, and the mountain smoking: and when the people saw it, they removed, and stood afar off.

- Shofars were blown on the Almighty's Sabbaths.

Psalm 81:3
Blow up the trumpet in the new moon, in the time appointed, on our solemn feast day.

Lev. 23:24
Speak unto the children of Israel, saying, In the seventh month, in the first day of the month, shall ye have a sabbath, a memorial of blowing of trumpets, an holy convocation.

Lev. 25:9
Then shalt thou cause the trumpet of the jubilee to sound on the tenth day of the seventh month, in the day of atonement shall ye make the trumpet sound throughout all your land.

- Shofars were blown when the walls at Jericho came down.

Josh. 6:4,5
And seven priests shall bear before the ark seven trumpets of rams' horns: and the seventh day ye shall compass the city seven times, and the priests shall blow

with the trumpets. 5: And it shall come to pass, that when they make a long blast with the ram's horn, and when ye hear the sound of the trumpet, all the people shall shout with a great shout; and the wall of the city shall fall down flat, and the people shall ascend up every man straight before him...

Josh. 6:20
So the people shouted when the priests blew with the trumpets: and it came to pass, when the people heard the sound of the trumpet, and the people shouted with a great shout, that the wall fell down flat, so that the people went up into the city, every man straight before him, and they took the city.

- Shofars were blown as a sign of victory in warfare.

Judg. 7:16
And he (Gideon) divided the three hundred men into three companies, and he put a trumpet in every man's hand, with empty pitchers, and lamps within the pitchers...

Judg. 7:20
And the three companies blew the trumpets, and brake the pitchers, and held the lamps in their left hands, and the trumpets in their right hands to blow withal: and they cried, The sword of the LORD, and of Gideon.

2 Chron. 13:12-15-
And, behold, God himself is with us for our captain, and his priests with sounding trumpets to cry alarm against you. O children of Israel, fight ye not against the LORD God of your fathers; for ye shall not prosper. 13: But Jeroboam caused an ambushment to come about behind them: so they were before Judah, and the ambushment was behind them. 14: And when Judah looked back, behold, the battle was before and behind: and they cried unto the LORD, and the priests sounded with the trumpets. 15: Then the men of Judah gave a shout: and as the men of Judah shouted, it came to pass, that God smote Jeroboam and all Israel before Abijah and Judah.

- Shofars were blown when the Ark of the Covenant was returned to Jerusalem.

> *2 Sam. 6:15*
> *So David and all the house of Israel brought up the ark of the LORD with shouting, and with the sound of the trumpet.*
>
> *Shofars were blown when King Solomon was anointed King.*
>
> *1 Kgs. 1:34*
> *And let Zadok the priest and Nathan the prophet anoint him there king over Israel: and blow ye with the trumpet, and say, God save king Solomon.*

- Shofars were blown when the temple was dedicated.

> *2 Chron. 5:13*
> *It came even to pass, as the trumpeters and singers were as one, to make one sound to be heard in praising and thanking the LORD; and when they lifted up their voice with the trumpets and cymbals and instruments of musick, and praised the LORD, saying, For he is good; for his mercy endureth for ever: that then the house was filled with a cloud, even the house of the LORD.*

- Shofars were blown when the temple was being rebuilt.

> *Neh. 4:18*
> *For the builders, every one had his sword girded by his side, and so builded. And he that sounded the trumpet was by me.*
>
> *Neh. 4:20*
> *In what place therefore ye hear the sound of the trumpet, resort ye thither unto us: our God shall fight for us.*

- Shofars were blown by the men guarding the people.

> *Ezek. 33:3-6*
> *If when he seeth the sword come upon the land, he blow the trumpet, and warn the people.; 4: Then whosoever heareth the sound of the trumpet, and taketh not warning; if the sword come, and take him away, his blood shall be upon his own head. 5: He heard the sound of the trumpet, and took not warning; his blood shall be upon him. But he that taketh warning shall deliver his soul. :6: But if the watchman see the sword come, and blow not the trumpet, and the people be*

not warned; if the sword come, and take any person from among them, he is
taken away in his iniquity; but his blood will I require at the watchman's hand.

- Shofars were blown to warn others about sin and its consequences.

Isa. 58:1
Cry aloud, spare not, lift up thy voice like a trumpet, and shew my people their
transgression, and the house of Jacob their sins.

Joel 2:1
Blow ye the trumpet in Zion, and sound an alarm in my holy mountain: let all
the inhabitants of the land tremble: for the day of the LORD cometh,
for it is nigh at hand.

- God will blow the shofar when He comes again.

Zech. 9:14
And the LORD shall be seen over them, and his arrow shall go forth as the
lightning: and the LORD GOD shall blow the trumpet,
and shall go with whirlwinds of the south.

Isa. 18:3
All ye inhabitants of the world, and dwellers on the earth, see ye, when he lifteth
up an ensign on the mountains; and when HE bloweth a trumpet, hear ye.

Isa. 27:13
And it shall come to pass in that day, that the GREAT trumpet shall be
blown, and they shall come which were ready to perish in the land of Assyria,
and the outcasts in the land of Egypt, and shall worship the
LORD in the holy mount at Jerusalem.

- Shofars were blown as a warning, but the people didn't listen.

We live in a world today that doesn't want to take warning. We live in a world today that doesn't want to hear truth. So when God speaks, sometimes it is a warning. God sends his watchmen, and they prophetically warn the body of Christ. Jeremiah was sent as a prophet of God, but they wouldn't listen to him. But Jeremiah was faithful and he listened to God and delivered the word of the Lord even when they didn't want to hear it.

> *Jer. 6:17*
> *Also I set watchmen over you, saying, Hearken to the sound of the trumpet.*
> *But they said, We will not hearken.*

The shofar is still an important part of Jewish worship today. If you attend any synagogue, you will hear the shofar being blown as part of their high holy days. It's used during the Feast of Trumpets on the Day of Atonement, and it's blown as a reminder of our covenant with God and the covenant that they have with him.

I think it's interesting that we tell our children in Sunday school about the story of Jericho and the walls coming down. Now, because of the archaeological studies in Israel, we have proof that there was a Jericho and there were walls surrounding that city. When they were walking around the city it was an act of faith. They walked around the walls and then blew the trumpet as an act of obedience. The power to cause those walls to fall didn't manifest until the seventh time around. Sometimes you just have to do things by faith.

When King David brought the Ark back to Jerusalem, the shofars accompanied him. It was King David announcing the return of the holy back to Jerusalem. He was doing it as a sign of his commitment to God. He worshipped God freely with all his might in front of the skeptics, and he didn't care what he looked like. He was demonstrating to the unbelievers that he was in covenant with God, and he was recommitting himself to God by faithfully bringing the Ark back.

When King Solomon was anointed King of Israel, the shofars were blown. It was symbolic of the dedication the Jewish people had to their new king. Solomon was a wise man, and blowing those shofars was symbolic of their following the anointed king.

Shofars are blown to call people to worship. They didn't have a church bell or cell phones or updates on their computers and email. They had a simple horn that could be heard throughout the city that announced it was time to come together to worship. When the temple was dedicated, the shofar was sounded to call the people together to worship. Coming together to worship God is something we're called to do corporately. When the Israelites returned from exile and they began to rebuild the city after their captivity, the shofars were blown. They blew them as a symbol that God was in the business of restoring his capital city and his people. The shofar is a symbol of restoration. It's a symbol of the new thing that God is going to do when he brings people back together.

The trumpet was also used by the watchmen, or the guards when they were protecting Zion. They had to have people up on the walls to let others know when the enemy was coming. The watchman's job was to alert those that were busy on the ground working that the enemy was coming and they had to prepare. When we blow shofars today, we are warning those around us to be aware and awake and to prepare for the potential of the demonic attack on our lives and the body of Christ as a whole.

The shofar is often likened unto a prophet. Prophets are intercessors. They stand in the gap for the people of God and they pray. They see what is coming by the spirit of God, and they reveal that to the people that they minister to. It's a form of divine protection. It warns the body to be prepared, organized, and alert. Don't you love it when God alerts you of an oncoming attack? I do. Prophets not only warn the people of potential attack, but the prophets also warned the body of sin and how it can destroy them.

When we blow our shofars today, we are calling people back to faith in God. We are crying out the need for repentance and obedience by the spirit of God. It's symbolic. We know that in the last days there will be a great trumpet that will sound. When this trumpet is blown, those who are dead in Christ will rise first and those who have been left behind will meet Jesus in the air. We are told that when we hear that trumpet sound, we will be gone to meet him in the air. And when we blow the ram's horns today, we are saying, "Get ready because Jesus is coming soon!" We must be ready. We've been told in the Scriptures we don't know what day or hour he is going to come. But if we keep our hearts right, we have nothing to fear. The sad part is that most people won't listen to the warnings given by prophets, preachers, friends, or other Christians. There are many things that are near and dear to God. He is drawn by broken, truthful, repentant, obedient, dedicated people. There is a judgment day that is coming. When the thousand-year millennial reign is over, God will come and judge the living and the dead at the white throne judgment. When you humble yourself and repent, you have nothing to fear. Just as the believers during Jeremiah's lifetime wouldn't listen to him, there are those that won't listen to you or to me. All we can do is sound the alarm and keep our lamps full. We are to be a light in a time of darkness. We are to declare His coming kingdom now.

CHAPTER 5

The Worship Leader

"You haven't prepared yourself for worship if you just practice musical art"
—LaMar Boschman, A Passion for His Presence

I long to be known as an extravagant worshiper...that God would discover the song in my heart to be elaborate, overgenerous, and wasteful in my pursuit of Him.
~ Darlene Zschech

Being a worship leader can be the most rewarding position in the world. Especially in the church today, it seems like the worship leader is the cool guy on the block. Everyone admires and looks up to the leader on the stage and the spotlight they are in. It can be a rewarding ministry, but if he or she is not careful, the visible position can crush you.

I would like to go back to the foundations or the fundamentals of being a worship leader and make sure that those are understood first. Understanding the function and role can make the job easier. The purpose of a worship leader is to inspire worship visually and audibly. Yes, it's a musical and technical position. However, it isn't just a musician who can play. It's a musician who visually can lead others by example into the presence of God. I like the way Worship Leader LaMar Boschman points out, "The goal of a worship leader is to help the church know, perceive, meet with, experience, see, sense, feel, be impressed with, be affected by, moved by and touched by the power of God's presence."[2]

Worship leaders must understand the mission of the worship team. Why do we sing and play the instruments the way that we do? And how does that relate to Christ and the Word of God? The band and ministers of music will stay focused if they understand why they do what they do.

Let's be clear: Not everybody is called to be a worship leader. Above all, he or she must have a huge heart for God. It also takes someone with a certain level of skill. Going through the process can be a difficult one. The process can take years. It's going to take discipline and hard work. How do you know if you're called to lead worship? Usually, there is a divine witness inside of you and you just know this is what you're supposed to do. It's your passion.

Because you have that witness inside you, the process will be joyful. Not necessarily easy, but joyful. Honestly, if you love leading worship, you also enjoy the rehearsal process and the fellowship that comes with working with other musicians. Is there some sort of a confirmation in your spirit that this is your calling? Because worship leaders are up in front of others, the ability is noticeable.

How do people respond to you when you lead worship? Are those around you in the church or the chapel responding to your leadership? It can be extremely frustrating and difficult when you're learning to do it. Bottom line is don't be hard on yourself. Try to enjoy the journey. The enemy can work on your mind and make you question yourself and doubt your ability. One of the greatest killers of calling and anointing is comparison. Musicians have a tendency to compare themselves all the time to others, and it's not right. We already have a Hillsong, Bethel, International House of Prayer, Jesus Culture or Elevation worship. We don't need another one. We need you to be you and to be uniquely you. When you're comfortable with yourself, your gifting, and your ability, it gets easier. When you are not in to comparisons, that's when you can truly be free on

---

[2] Boschman, LaMar. World Leaders Training Course (1993).

the platform. The bottom line is that you're not there to please other people; you are there to minister to the Lord first.

Do you feel His pleasure when you minister to him? When you are alone one-on-one with God singing and ministering to Him, how does that feel spiritually? When you feel His pleasure, His presence, joy or satisfaction, that's where the call to be a worship leader starts. When you find it personally and spiritually fulfilling, it's a good indicator that you're called to lead worship.

If you're called to lead worship, you should feel the grace of God on your life to do it. There will be grace upon you and upon others while you're learning. Is it something that seems natural? Is it something that is fulfilling? Is it important to you?

Life is just a breath. We have a short amount of time to live. What do you do with that time? If you spend your time ministering to the Lord, that's a good indication that you're called to be a worship leader.

Have you ever asked the Lord, "What do You want to me to do?" It seems to me at this point in my life I'm asking him that question now more than ever. In fact, writing this book is part of my obedience to Him. There are things in life that I know I was born to accomplish. Teaching and training others is a big part of that call.

I also think it's important if you're going to lead worship that you have a heart for the people. Worship leaders must love the local church. They must love the leaders of that church. They must feel a burden or responsibility to see the people come into the presence of God. Do you want to make a difference in the lives of others? Do you want to do something that has eternal value? Do you want to live a life of purpose and meaning that's bigger than you? Are you willing to serve other musicians that you're working with?

For me, the real indicator of a true worship leader is the student that carefully and prayerfully prepares for everyone else in the band. They make sure all the musicians that they are working with have time to prepare music and to learn the music. If you don't have anybody following you, you're not a leader. Leaders care for and serve others. Good leaders think about the people they play with. They want them to feel fulfilled and comfortable. They want the training process to be organized and thought out. They serve others by making all band members sound good – even those who may play at different levels musically. No one wants to look or sound bad on the platform. Taking care of others musically and spiritually is part of that process.

Don't get caught up in your skill level when you get started. God has a way of taking your skill level or where you are right now and multiplying it when you give it to Him. I can't tell you how many outstanding guitar players I worked with over the years who are not comfortable singing. But when I get them in a room with a group of other men and I get them working on vocal technique, they realize they really can sing. All they need is some basic training, encouragement, and support.

On the other hand, I have outstanding vocalists who have no concept of what it is to play. They know just one thing. They are concerned with how they sound and they want the band to follow them. They don't understand the technical problems that musicians have. It's going to take a lot of time and experience to get different people at different places to understand and support each other, but it's very important. The bottom line is that if you are called to be a worship leader, grace will sustain while you are in the learning process. So relax and try to enjoy the journey. I am convinced that God loves watching the journey. He loves it when broken, humble musicians are dependent on Him and therefore give Him all of the honor and the glory. I have seen the presence of God fall hard in chapels with the most humble, broken, heartfelt worship leader and the simplest set. God will share his glory with no one.

Christ is always the focus of everything we do. Our goal is to encounter Christ. Music is going to be the means or the way we get into His presence. Our job is to bring the people into the presence of the Lord through the worship. It's not about the songs or even the worship; it's all about Him. Now don't get me wrong: The musical part is important. If the music is not done well, it can be a big distraction and can keep people from coming into God's presence. I always say that the band that the Holy Spirit uses is the band that gets out of God's way. When the Holy

Spirit is directing a service, that's when you know it's a good set or a powerful service.

Worship leaders are to take the body of Christ from the outer courts into the holy of holies. Many years ago I did the tabernacle of Moses production at my school. Students had to learn how the Levitical priests had to enter the gates of the tabernacle. They learned all of the parts of the Tabernacle of Moses and how to move through each of the stations. The final destination was the Holy of Holies. Worship is a journey. Worship leaders today are called of God to help people go on spiritual journey. We start with praise at the gates with thanksgiving in our hearts. Thanksgiving is so powerful. The Holy Spirit knows and honors a thankful heart and a thankful congregation. We start a service or a meeting with all of the things going on in our lives and we by choice put those things down and begin to worship. When we go on this spiritual journey we offer our sacrifices of praise. When we do the supernatural, the holy presence of God comes. God is always with us. But we begin to change our focus. We go from being self-conscious to God conscious. Worship is a journey. Our job as worship leaders is to help the congregation, the instrumentalists and the singers go on that journey with us. Leaders know where they're going. They have a plan and they work that plan. The band easily follows the leader. The Holy Spirit can move from that plan, but that usually comes from music that is well known and rehearsed.

I am a teacher and I believe in good lesson plans. When we're pulling sets, we are thinking about a multitude of things. We are carefully planning the worship journey. Do the tempos work together? Are the keys correct for the band and the vocals? Can the people who are coming sing with you? Do the keys easily connect? When I am working with rookie leaders, we do the entire set in the key of G or D. They are connected and related. They modulate easily. Then I will add another key like A. From that I introduce the circle of 5ths and the Nashville chord system.

The worship leader should look for an opportunity to lead the body and the band into another spiritual dimension or to step across or over into prophetic worship. This is when the Holy Spirit takes control of the set. New music is created and is spontaneous. I'm thankful when I have seasoned musicians who can move prophetically under the leading and the guiding of the Holy Spirit. But that comes with time and study of the Nashville chord system.

Real worship is not about what comes out of the speakers, but it's what's in the hearts of the worshippers. I was reminded of this one day when I was discouraged over a sound system not working. Several of our new speakers had been blown the Wednesday night before. Someone who didn't know how run the sound. A good sound man is so important. Our chapel was getting ready to start, and I was discouraged and frustrated. On that day, one of our principals encouraged me. He told me the story of how he had smuggled Bibles behind the Iron Curtain and had had many supernatural encounters taking these Bibles to places where it was illegal to own one. He told me about the passionate worship after he had delivered the Bibles to the secret underground meeting places. In many of these places, the people were not allowed to sing. If they had been heard singing, they could have all been arrested and thrown in jail. They had to worship with their whole heart and with their mind in silence for fear of being heard. It was the most passionate worship experiences that he ever heard. I'm thankful for him and for his life. And I've never forgotten that the most powerful worship is often experienced in silence. So remember that the next time you're in a similar situation and allow the Lord to have His way in your worship.

Tempos are important as well. There's nothing worse than a song played at the wrong tempo or a song that is played too slow. A good drummer can make or break your band. Frankly, the rhythm section is vital to a good worship band or set. Tempos can be set correctly by the acoustic or keyboard player at the beginning of a song, and then the drummer can come in. When we are planning a worship set, I ask my students, "What is the theme of the set? Does this theme or the lyrics in the song connect? Does the worship journey feel like it's going somewhere? Are there key words that connect the songs together?" For instance, Rain, Fire, Blood, Holy Spirit or Name of Jesus.

Style is also an important element. If you have two contrasting styles, it may not flow together easily. Different styles have different tempos, and that usually means a clean break between songs.

Every worship leader must work the rough spots in a worship set. Each set has them. Transitions must be short or fluid. If the transitions are done well, you shouldn't even notice them. When you notice them, that's when you know the trouble. Transitions must be rehearsed just like the songs are rehearsed. The entire band should work as a team to cover those transitions and to make sure they flow. Hand signals and body language help as well as visual cues. There's nothing wrong with going into chorus of the next song instead of the verse. Nothing wrong shaking the order of the songs. When you shake up the order of the song, it can feel totally spontaneous, but in reality, it's planned and prepared by the band, and everyone is on board working that plan.

A good worship leader will organize the sequence of events and, if possible, communicate what's going to happen to the pastoral staff or special speaker. Good communication puts everyone at ease. When pastors understand why things are done, it helps them, too. Most churches today are dependent on paid staff and volunteers. If the volunteers are frustrated, they won't stay long.

A good worship leader must be a worshiper first. If they have a passion for the presence of the Lord, you can see it in the congregation. You know when a worship leader loves the presence of the Lord. It's a joyful thing. When you are crying out to God and his presence comes, it's a joyful, rewarding thing. There is no greater satisfaction.

It's impossible to lead others where you have not been yourself. It's so important to spend time in God's presence. When you know where God is found, you can take the people there.

Generally speaking, if the worship leader will press into the presence of God, then he or she can take the body of Christ with him or her. Your destination is the presence and glory of God. What the man of God does with the presence is up to him. But the worship leader must do his job to get the people there.

Good worship leaders have to be prepared. You have to know the music before the rehearsal starts. This is extremely hard on young people who want to do a lot of new music. One year we decided to learn over 80 new worship choruses. Honestly, it was a miserable year because we were always learning something new. New songs are great, and I love learning new music, but you should always work with older, more familiar songs. If your congregation is always learning new material, it's hard to shut down the brain and focus on the presence of the Lord and what He is saying to you. I love the rehearsal process. I love hanging with musicians. But if the rehearsal is a good one, you will feel the pleasure and the presence of the Lord.

I always tell my students that a good rehearsal is spent on the music. It's not talking about the music; it's actually playing and thinking. How much time you actually play in rehearsal is a good indicator of how good the rehearsal really is. But the worship leader must know that music before the rehearsal start. And that rehearsal always takes place at home. That private rehearsal and practice is truly a way of serving the band. When a worship leader walks into a rehearsal and is prepared, everyone enjoys the rehearsal process. Everyone loves to get it done. Preparation for rehearsal is the best way to serve those you play with. Loving them, caring for them means being prepared.

The bottom line is that leaders must have a servant's heart that serves, waits on, or attends to their musicians. As a worship leader you wait on the Lord, and you want to do his will in each service. You carefully consider what the body of Christ needs to hear or sing, and you wait on them and consider what they need in the service. The goal is to bring them together in God's presence.

Worship leaders constantly monitor and are involved with people – even during the service itself. The concern should be focused on the people more than on the music. Jesus Christ gave his life for the music. It's all about the people, and it's all about Him.

In my opinion all worship leaders should be prophetic in nature. When we are planning praise and worship services, we are asking the Lord what is coming. We are praying and asking God to give us direction and confirmation. All of that is prophetic in nature. The worship leader must go out ahead of the people and ask the Holy Spirit where He wants the service to God. You will know he is going to move in a different direction based on what you feel or sense in the rehearsal. As the rehearsal goes, so goes the meeting. If you feel nothing, it may mean that you have the wrong set or God is going to do something and you have not figured that out yet.

Prayer is the key to being led by the Holy Spirit. Good worship leaders must have a solid prayer life. Being sensitive to the Holy Spirit comes in private times of worship and prayer.

How do you begin to prepare for your calling?

Start at home with your family or your close friends. Start small and intimate. That's not intimidating. Almost every worship leader I know started out in a small group or a small youth group or Bible study. Do not despise the days of small beginnings. Grant and I ministered every Sunday at an assisted living complex for 11 years. The kids sang with me. I have some amazing memories from that time. My kids were so precious. They understood how important Jesus was to their father and me. We led by example. We learned to be prepared for Sundays. The kids learned how to stand up in front of others and share their personal stories. They often were not very prepared but knew that their daddy expected them to speak or sing, and they usually picked something from school or children's church. The older they got, the smarter they got, and they would preach sermons from their notes from church. One time, Josiah took up an offering. He said to the sweet elderly people one Sunday, "God wants to bless you. And if you give him your pennies, God will give you quarters." Well, those darling people dug down in their pockets that day and gave quarters to my sweet little man. He will never forget it. My children learned to love older people and how to be kind. They learned how to listen and they learned that life is short and you must be prepared for eternity. My sweet little boy prayed the sinner's prayer with several people before they went home to heaven. He is a great kid, and he can lead others into God's presence.

They learned all of that by doing. Ministry is something you do together. You don't have to have a large platform or a lot of people looking at you. It's not about the sound system or the lighting. Ministry is one-on-one with people. Ministry is simple its listening to people and loving people. It was an important time in the history of our family. I would not trade those years for anything. We have some funny memoires from those days, but we also have some sacred ones, too.

Learning to lead is a process. Take time to listen to and study other worship leaders. Listen to their music and their style. Listen to worship leaders teach. I love to listen to Bethel's Worship U. The leaders at Bethel are such strong believers. They have a solid biblical foundation for what they do. They are humble, down-to-earth people who love each other like family. I also like to listen to worship leaders on YouTube. Start somewhere, stay faithful and see your gifting grow.

Practice music at home

I highly recommend that you play along with musicians. Get a chord chart and play along with people playing the same thing on YouTube or in recording. It will give you a sense of tempo and when the chord changes are correct. Remember you will be playing live with a band, and it's not all about you. You are a piece of the puzzle, and you must fit musically with where the band is going. Listen to other musicians. Developing your musical ear is vital to your ministry.

Another way of evaluating what you're doing is recording what you are playing and listen to it. Recordings don't lie. They can tell you how you really sound. I will record my choirs and ensembles before competitions so they can hear the mistakes. When they hear how it really sounds out front, they understand what I am trying to tell them, and they are supportive of the changes I am trying to make and how to fix them.

It's equally important that instrumentalists understand how to sing. A good instrumentalist will have compassion on vocalists. In the same way, I think it's important for vocalists also to be musicians. When they understand how difficult it is at times for the players, a good vocalist will do all they can to understand, work with, and support the band. When you understand and you talk it out, it eliminates frustration. Frustration ends where communication begins.

I am a classically trained musician. I train vocalists to sing classical choral technique. It's so important that vocalists don't hurt themselves. Vocalists have only one instrument, and it cannot be replaced. Vocalists can damage their voice and have to have several months of vocal rest. You must be careful and not hurt yourself. Yelling or screaming in worship is not necessary. Especially not today with modern technology and microphones. There's NO reason to yell. You can do enormous damage to your voice and destroy your ministry if you get nodes. Nodes are scar tissue that forms on the vocal cords that eliminate certain spots in your vocal range. Nodes are devastating to any vocalist. Often surgery and total vocal rest is necessary. Do not sing on a bad cold or when you have postnasal drip. That drainage will land on your vocal cords and damage them. Even in the middle of a long praise and worship set, it's vital that the vocalist rest, hydrate and not talk. Vocalists, you must protect your instrument just like a good guitar player protects his guitar.

Worship leaders must protect themselves. Leaders that don't sleep or eat well will eventually feel it in their body. Vocalists must take Vitamin C and a multivitamin to keep themselves healthy. It's also important that vocalists stay in shape aerobically. Running or jogging, keeping your breath control strong, will help you sing on pitch and give you stamina.

Guard your heart with all diligence

Lastly, I'm very careful to guard myself emotionally and spiritually. My state of mind and spirit is reflected on how I sound and how I lead. No matter what is going on in life, you are going to have challenges. Life can deal you some hard things. No matter what I am going through, I feel it in my music. Music touches me in the deepest part of who I am. I know that no matter how I feel, He is worthy of my praise. It's in His presence that I get the strength to go on and continue to pursue ministry. The ministry at times can be heart breaking. People come and go. But Jesus is always the same. His presence should be your safe place. The place you run to for comfort and peace. The anointing always increases in my life when I forgive others and don't allow bitterness into my heart. Staying flexible and humble will help you guard your heart. God has a way of protecting and guarding those who love Him. But before God can defend or protect us, we have to allow Him to do a deep work in our heart, and we must protect that place.

CHAPTER 6

Prophetic Worship

*Beautiful music is the art of the prophets
that can calm the agitations of the soul;
it is one of the most magnificent and delightful presents God has given us.*
~Martin Luther

And when the musician played, the hand of the Lord came upon him.
2 Kings 3:15

*As Prophetic Musicians we are not trying to escape this world
but we are wanting to help make sense of it,
Music is one of the most powerful ways to impact a human heart
and now more than ever people need to
hear and feel Gods heart, through Music.*
~Misti Edwards

The Holy Spirit wants to speak through worship leaders. He is raising up a generation of praise and worship leaders that will not just follow the verse chorus structure but will also flow in the Holy Spirit. Prophetic worship sets captives free.

We see all throughout Scripture where people were moved to prophesy under an anointing when musical instruments were included. I so enjoy the portion of Scripture out of First Samuel 10:5-6 where the prophets and the musical instruments work and walk together:

> *... And it will happen, when you have come there to the city, that you will meet a group of prophets coming down from the high place with a stringed instrument, a tambourine, a flute, and a harp before them; and they will be prophesying. Then the Spirit of the LORD will come upon you, and you will prophesy with them ...*

Old Testament prophets always worked or traveled in conjunction with musicians. When the Spirit of God would fall on them, they would prophesy. We see another example in First Chronicles 25 where the musicians would "prophesy with harps, stringed instruments, and cymbals" (verse 1). In the same chapter, the six sons of Jeduthun "prophesied with a harp to give thanks and to praise the Lord" (verse 3). Many of these musicians sang under the inspiration of God. So this was common in Old Testament times for music and prophecy to work together.

The prophetic gift of music is helping the body of Christ in a similar way in today's worship services. Because we live in the New Covenant, the Holy Spirit dwells in us. When the Holy Spirit is moving in a worship service, we get His direction and His heart. The Holy Spirit will manifest and function through many people in various ways. More and more musicians are prophesying on their instruments by playing under the inspiration of the Holy Spirit. The sound on their instruments releases the anointing over people. An anointed musician's highest reward is playing by the spirit over others and watching the Holy Spirit help set them free. This free prophetic flow will inspire prophets and believers alike to move in the gifts of the spirit.

What is a prophetic musician?

Prophetic worship is listening to God's heart and playing music or singing songs that come from the throne of God. It's when the musician becomes a prophetic voice. He sings into the atmosphere and brings heaven to earth through sound, accompanied by melody or music. According to *Smith's Bible Dictionary*, a prophet is "one who announces or pours forth the declarations of God." The Greek word, *prophētēs* (προφητης), goes further in describing this person as "one who speaks for another, especially one who speaks for a god, and so interprets his will to man."[3] Prophesying is all about ministering under the inspiration of the Holy Spirit. It's a natural talent or ability that flows from the musician's heart. When the musician cooperates with the purposes of God to express God's Word and what God wants to do and how he wants to move, Holy Spirit inspired music will follow.

Strong's Dictionary further defines the word "prophecy" as "flowing abundantly, to utter, or belch out, to pour out, send forth, utter."[4] A musician that is allowed to foster or develop these prophetic gifts can learn over time to yield to the Holy Spirit in such a way that the Word of the Lord comes out of his instruments or from his singing voice. You can hear the Holy Spirit singing through the psalmist of the Lord. You can hear what the Holy Spirit wants to do. When that is happening, Jesus will manifest in our hearts and our lives. The church will grow and will be edified.

A prophetic musician perceives music and ministry a little bit differently. A prophetic musician understands all of the musical tasks that must be done but sees music as a means for releasing the supernatural. Prophetic music will encourage, comfort, strengthen and edify people. By nature, it will encourage Christians to step into a higher level of prayer and worship. Prophetic musicians play until an anointed, spirit-led song is released, and in that moment the worship leader can pick up the heartbeat of God.

The Holy Spirit brings revelation to the worshipers through songs which brings peace, joy, inspiration, and tears as the Holy Spirit speaks. It can happen two different ways. It can happen musically where an instrument is played and the melody brings revelation by the spirit to the person listening. Or it can come in the form of a song that is sung under the inspiration of the Holy Spirit. In order to operate in these ways, musicians must have an understanding of chord structure. The musician will have

[3] *Smith's Bible Dictionary: Comprising Antiquities, Biography, Geography, Natural History, Archaeology and Literature.* J M. Fuller 1893, Wordsearch10.com.

[4] *Strong's Dictionary.* Miklal Software Solutions, 2011.

many scriptures memorized and will have spent time in the Word knowing the character and nature of God. The Word of God sung under inspiration will bring the Glory of God in a prayer group or meeting.

This musical glory realm is where the Holy Spirit moves in the heart of the listener. As we listen intently while the musicians play, we can pick up the heartbeat of God that is illuminated to our spirit man.

Music is one of the most powerful tools that we have against darkness. Musicians that are consecrated can literally pull people out of darkness into light through the music. When you get spirit-led musicians who can play prophetically and you encourage them to play over an individual, you have the most powerful weapon of warfare available. Often it's not the musician's skill set, but it is the spiritual heart of discernment that that musician operates in that sets someone free. I call these musicians the "psalmists of the Lord." They won't just play some nice, cute choruses that entertain. They sing and decree light into darkness and set the captives free. This is the ultimate role of a ministering musician. This is a spiritual form of communication that transcends all other forms of communication. It's more meaningful than words. It's a pure form of communication of the heart and the mind. In many ways it's difficult to understand or even write about until you've experienced it. There is a depth to this type of worship that no dictionary or textbook can begin to capture.

Change in the Atmosphere

True prophetic music ministry will take us into the very presence of God. It will enable us to empower other people. But it has to be the right kind of music. This music must work in conjunction with the Holy Spirit. The anointing of God rides on music or sound. Have you ever noticed how an anointed instrument can literally change the spiritual atmosphere? Businesses understand the importance of music. When I walk into shops or stores, I pay attention to the music in the background. Retail stores know it sets the atmosphere of the place where you're shopping.

King David understood the power of praise and worship. King David was the least likely of all of his brothers to be the next King of Israel, but

God knew his heart. He played his harp one-on-one alone with God while he was tending to the sheep and no one was looking at him. He wasn't looking for a stage or a position; he was ministering unto the Lord. He had a relationship with God that was very strong. He ministered to the Lord. He knew God and loved him, and the Lord would come and dwell in his praises. David knew that the presence of God brought blessing, strength, and peace.

When King Saul tried to do things his way instead of following God's protocol and instructions, it opened him up for torment. Saul was desperate for peace. In fact, he was so distressed that he called in David, a young sheepherder, to play his harp because David had a reputation among the king's servants of being "skillful in playing, a mighty man of valor, a man of war, prudent in speech, and a handsome person; and the LORD is with him" (1 Sam. 16:18). David was brought in to change the atmosphere through music. As this sheep-farmer-turned-psalmist of the Lord played his instrument, the evil spirits left King Saul.

It's interesting in this portion of Scripture that the distressing spirit would leave Saul. When an anointed musician plays, it can drive darkness out of the lives of people who are coming to church to be set free. It's the job or the role of the minister of music to establish the spiritual atmosphere in such a way that those that are lost and hurting and broken can be delivered.

Prophets and Music

Prophetic people understand the importance of music. We see this very clearly in the life of Elisha the prophet. The kings of Edom, Israel, and Judah had brought all their fighting men together to go after the Moabites. For seven days they marched toward Moab but found no water for their animals or their armies to drink. That's a big problem when you're going to war against another tribe or nation. The king of Israel wimped out and said, "We're all going to die!" But Jehoshaphat, King of Judah, asked for a prophet to get them out of their situation. Elisha was called and asked for the harpist to come and play so that he could prophesy:

> *...Then it happened, when the musician played, that the hand of the*
> LORD *came upon him.*
> [16] *And he said, "Thus says the* LORD: *'Make this valley full of ditches.'*
> [17] *For thus says the* LORD: *'You shall not see wind, nor shall you see rain;*
> *yet that valley shall be filled with water, so that you, your cattle,*
> *and your animals may drink.'*
> [18] *And this is a simple matter in the sight of the* LORD;
> *He will also deliver the Moabites into your hand.*
> [19] *Also you shall attack every fortified city and every choice city, and shall cut*
> *down every good tree, and stop up every spring of water, and ruin every good*
> *piece of land with stones."*
>
> *2 King 3:15-19*

Not only did Elisha tell them how to they would get water, but he also gave specific directions about how to defeat the Moabites. Did the musician bring the prophecy, or did the prophet hear from the Lord? I say it was both. The anointing on the musical instrument played at the right time brought about the word from the Lord through the prophet. That's the power of prophetic music and worship!

As New Testament Christians, we can fully operate in the gifts of the spirit by the Holy Spirit. That means at times musically we can operate in words of knowledge and wisdom, and we can sing these words over others. Have you ever seen a prophet sing under the inspiration of the Holy Ghost over a believer? It's so powerful! It's an unforgettable experience. The same spirit of God that's inside of me is inside of everyone else. That's why if you have a praise and worship band operating in agreement, they all can be flowing in the same direction prophetically.

As Dr. Hamon writes in *Apostles, Prophets, and the Coming Moves of God,* "God is preparing His Church to become an invincible, unstoppable, unconquerable, overcoming Army of the Lord that subdues everything under Christ's feet. There will be a sovereign restorational move of God to activate all that is needed for His army to be and do what He has eternally purposed. The generals who will lead this army will be those who have progressively been prepared by incorporating every restorational truth into their life and ministry."[5]

In the days coming we are going to have to be careful that we don't play with worship. I loved Pastor Billy Joe Daugherty dearly. I will never forget one afternoon when he stopped by my room to talk about praise and worship at school. He told me that he would rather have one student on the stage whose heart was right than have a bunch of students who were skillful whose hearts were wrong. I will never forget it. He wasn't interested in a bunch of flashy music in Chapel. What he wanted were kids whose hearts were right for God because he understood biblically that if their hearts were right, the anointing would flow in Chapel. I tried the best I could over the years to mentor and train musicians and give them an opportunity to minister. Inevitably what was in the heart of the student came out of them on the platform.

It's time for the songs of the Lord to be sung by the next generation of ministers of music. It's time for the next generation of prophetic worship leaders to rise up and to sing with their instruments and voices. There is a generation of Holy Ghost born-again spirit filled musicians that are going to sing decree and play the word of the Lord. They are called to pull people out of darkness into light. They are called by God to be a light and to draw people to the King of kings and the Lord of lords. Lord, release your prophetic anointing on this generation!

---

[5] Hamon, Bill. *Apostles, Prophets, and the Coming Moves of God.* Destiny Image, 1997, p. 251.

Music is the art of the prophets and the gift of God.

~Martin Luther

"Whenever His people gather and worship Him,
God promises He will make His
presence known in their midst.
On the other hand, where God's people consistently
neglect true spiritual worship,
His manifest presence is rarely experienced."

~Ralph Mahoney

CHAPTER 7

When Praise is a Sacrifice

"God requires your sacrifice of praise, at precisely what seems like the worst moment, because it reveals Christ Jesus in your life."
~*Terry Law, The Power of Praise and Worship*

The cancer wing of St. Luke's Hospital in Sioux City, Iowa, is a hard memory for me. I had rushed home quickly knowing my mother was very ill. I didn't want to face it. She'd made a decision to have an additional aggressive surgery to remove the cancer. My heart was broken. Looking back at it now, I think I was in denial. I just could not comprehend losing my mother.

When something is so painful that you can't face it, you might put it in a back corner in your mind knowing you'll deal with it later. I understand grief. It goes so deep that it's hard to function. Or think normally.

It was during that week in the hospital that I learned an important lesson about praise and worship. When you worship and it hurts to worship, He meets you. When you choose to sing when you don't feel like singing, but you understand that God is the answer to your problem, you are comforted. When you sing to Him in a broken state of mind, He gives you grace and strength. I felt His presence so strong. Looking back at it, in a strange kind of way, I appreciate the experience. It truly was supernatural how God came to me in such a powerful way and reassured me with such a deep comfort. The power and presence of God that manifested around me was so tangible.

There were specific moments about my mom's passing that are precious to me. My mother was a great singer. The one thing she wanted to live for was her granddaughter. We had some amazing moments in the hospital with my daughter before she left this earth. She prayed over each of us and spoke a blessing over each of us. It meant so much to my children. I also saw her reaction when under heavy medication she couldn't communicate in any way, shape, or form, but she could hear. And the one thing that she could hear more acutely than anything else was the voice of my beautiful daughter singing to her. She wanted to watch Jenava grow up and be a successful woman. But in that painful moment, the most comforting thing, the most beautiful thing, was worship. I remember singing to myself. I remember singing before the funeral. Terry Law wrote the book, *The Power of Praise and Worship*. In this book, he shares the heartbreaking story of losing his wife Jan in the early years of their marriage. In the book he talks about worshiping in the night hours – not because he felt like it, but because the Lord told him to. He knew that if he could praise and worship through his grief that he could find strength to go on living. The testimony out of that book has always ministered to me. That revelation is what carried me through the season of losing my mother. We always praise God. Not because we feel like it, but because he is worthy. Real praise doesn't have anything to do with what we like or what we don't like. It has to do with His worth.

Hebrews 13:15
15 Therefore by Him let us continually offer the sacrifice of praise to God, that is, the fruit of our lips, giving thanks to His name.

Psalm 34:1
1 A Psalm of David when he pretended madness before Abimelech, who drove him away, and he departed. I will bless the LORD at all times; His praise shall continually be in my mouth.

I love the study notes on Psalm 34. King David was pretending to be mad. And in the middle of this difficult situation, he made the choice to worship God. Life is difficult. No matter what you do or no matter how much you try to honor God and live an honorable life, there are going to be ups and downs. There are going to be moments of incredible joy and of unbelievable heartbreak. The good news is you don't have to go through it alone. You can hold onto something that is bigger and stronger than you. You hold on to the things that will truly give you peace and comfort when your heart is breaking in two. When I study Scripture, it always amazes me the horrific things men and women of God went through. The people in the Bible were real and they suffered enormously. But in the middle of that pain and suffering, God would show up for them in unusual ways.

Acts 16:22-26
22 Then the multitude rose up together against them; and the magistrates tore off their clothes and commanded them to be beaten with rods.
23 And when they had laid many stripes on them, they threw them into prison, commanding the jailer to keep them securely.
24 Having received such a charge, he put them into the inner prison and fastened their feet in the stocks.
25 But at midnight Paul and Silas were praying and singing hymns to God, and the prisoners were listening to them.
26 Suddenly there was a great earthquake, so that the foundations of the prison were shaken; and immediately all the doors were opened and everyone's chains were loosed.

God is so faithful. These men were in jail. Their feet and hands were in stocks. They had no way out. But when they began to sing and praise God, the door swung open and they were set free. God brought supernatural intervention in their deepest despair.

2 Chronicles 17:3-6
3 Now the LORD was with Jehoshaphat, because he walked in the former ways of his father David; he did not seek the Baals,
4 but sought the God of his father, and walked in His commandments and not according to the acts of Israel.

⁵ Therefore the LORD established the kingdom in his hand; and all Judah gave presents to Jehoshaphat, and he had riches and honor in abundance.
⁶ And his heart took delight in the ways of the LORD; moreover he removed the high places and wooden images from Judah.

When you seek God with all of your heart, you'll be given supernatural favor. Even if you are surrounded by others in occult practices.

2 Chronicles 20:6-9
⁶ and said: "O LORD God of our fathers, are You not God in heaven, and do You not rule over all the kingdoms of the nations, and in Your hand is there not power and might, so that no one is able to withstand You?
⁷ Are You not our God, who drove out the inhabitants of this land before Your people Israel, and gave it to the descendants of Abraham Your friend forever?
⁸ And they dwell in it, and have built You a sanctuary in it for Your name, saying,
⁹ If disaster comes upon us--sword, judgment, pestilence, or famine--we will stand before this temple and in Your presence (for Your name is in this temple), and cry out to You in our affliction, and You will hear and save.'

Crying out to God when you are enduring persecution will give you power and strength to endure. You see, the people of God gathered together and worshiped in the holy place together. They cried out to God and God heard them. As worship leaders, that's what we do. We gather the believers together and we lead worship. We enable them to pray and to sing and to worship corporately. We know according to the Word of God that in the last days it's going to get dark. Sin and evil are going to abound. We know the believers are going to experience enormous persecution. But because of Jesus and because of worship, we can come together and find strength and power in his presence.

2 Chronicles 20:15-23
¹⁵ And he said, "Listen, all you of Judah and you inhabitants of Jerusalem, and you, King Jehoshaphat! Thus says the LORD to you: 'Do not be afraid nor dismayed because of this great multitude, for the battle is not yours, but God's.

*16 Tomorrow go down against them. They will surely come up by the Ascent of
Ziz, and you will find them at the end of the brook
before the Wilderness of Jeruel.
17 You will not need to fight in this battle. Position yourselves, stand still and
see the salvation of the LORD, who is with you, O Judah and Jerusalem!' Do
not fear or be dismayed; tomorrow go out against them,
for the LORD is with you."
18 And Jehoshaphat bowed his head with his face to the ground, and all Judah
and the inhabitants of Jerusalem bowed before the LORD,
worshiping the LORD.
19 Then the Levites of the children of the Kohathites and of the children of the
Korahites stood up to praise the LORD God of Israel
with voices loud and high.
20 So they rose early in the morning and went out into the Wilderness of Tekoa;
and as they went out, Jehoshaphat stood and said, "Hear me, O Judah and you
inhabitants of Jerusalem: Believe in the LORD your God, and you shall be established; believe His prophets, and you shall prosper."
21 And when he had consulted with the people, he appointed those who should
sing to the LORD, and who should praise the beauty of holiness, as they went
out before the army and were saying: "Praise the LORD,
For His mercy endures forever."
22 Now when they began to sing and to praise, the LORD set ambushes against
the people of Ammon, Moab, and Mount Seir, who had come against Judah;
and they were defeated.
23 For the people of Ammon and Moab stood up against the inhabitants of
Mount Seir to utterly kill and destroy them. And when they had made an end
of the inhabitants of Seir, they helped to destroy one another.*

This was a difficult and dark time in Israel's history. But the people of God were given a promise. If they would listen to the prophets and do what they said, they would prosper. They organized the singers went ahead of the Army. Praise and worship is the highest form of spiritual warfare. When you invite God in worship, He will go ahead of you and fight your battles for you. When God is fighting for you, who can stand against you?

*Psalm 149:4-9
4 For the LORD takes pleasure in His people; He will beautify   the
humble with salvation.
5 Let the saints be joyful in glory; Let them sing aloud on their beds.
6 Let the high praises of God be in their mouth, And a two-edged sword in their*

> *hand,*
> *⁷ To execute vengeance on the nations, And punishments on the peoples;*
> *⁸ To bind their kings with chains, And their nobles with fetters of iron;*
> *⁹ To execute on them the written judgment-- This honor have all His saints.*
> *Praise the LORD!*

Have you ever thought of your praises being like a sword? Better yet, it's a two-edged sword in your hand when you worship God. Not only is it an aggressive weapon in one direction, but when you swing that weapon in another direction it's just as powerful. God says through your praise, He will deal with people, nations, and kings. He is your defender.

When you read Scriptures like that, it just makes you wonder why people don't spend a lot more time in praise and worship. If Christians really understood how God wants to fight their battles for them, they would never want to miss the worship part of the service. Oh, you know those stragglers who come in late. They come in on the last song just before the announcements. They are missing what God wants to do for them in their worship. When I get really busy and distracted but I have important decisions to make, the last thing in the world that I have time to do is to go to the piano and worship God in the middle of my battle. And yet when I do it, that's where I'm refreshed, empowered, and able to go on. When you know that praise is where your strength comes from, then that's the place you run to fastest.

> *Isaiah 30:27-32*
> *²⁷ Behold, the name of the LORD comes from afar, Burning with His anger,*
> *And His burden is heavy; His lips are full of indignation,*
> *And His tongue like a devouring fire.*
> *²⁸ His breath is like an overflowing stream, Which reaches up to the neck, To sift the nations with the sieve of futility; And there shall be a bridle in the jaws of the people, Causing them to err.*
> *²⁹ You shall have a song As in the night when a holy festival is kept, And gladness of heart as when one goes with a flute, To come into the mountain of the LORD, To the Mighty One of Israel.*
> *³⁰ The LORD will cause His glorious voice to be heard, And show the descent of His arm, With the indignation of His anger And the flame of a devouring fire, With scattering, tempest, and hailstones.*

> *31 For through the voice of the LORD Assyria will be beaten down,*
> *As He strikes with the rod.*
> *32 And in every place where the staff of punishment passes, Which the LORD*
> *lays on him, It will be with tambourines and harps;*
> *And in battles of brandishing He will fight with it.*

You have to admit this is a really fun portion of Scripture. God's offensive weapons according to Scripture are tambourines and harps, or our modern drums sets and acoustic guitars. There's something very aggressive about worship. When you aggressively fight in the spirit realm through worship, that's where God moves on your behalf. God wants to fight your battles, but what happens when you don't show up and fight? What happens when you get too busy to worship? What happens when you don't invite God into the situation? I look back at my life and realize there are so many times I missed it. I missed it because I didn't invite God into my battle, and He wants to fight them. Yes, He is sovereign, omnipotent, and omniscient, and He watches over me like His eyes are on the sparrow. But it's another thing for me to invite Him in the situation and to ask him to fight for me. I just wonder how many other spiritual battles could've been fought or won more quickly if I had been obedient.

> *Revelation 19:6-10*
> *6 And I heard, as it were, the voice of a great multitude, as the sound of many*
> *waters and as the sound of mighty thunderings, saying, "*
> *Alleluia! For the Lord God Omnipotent reigns!*
> *7 Let us be glad and rejoice and give Him glory, for the marriage of the Lamb*
> *has come, and His wife has made herself ready."*
> *8 And to her it was granted to be arrayed in fine linen, clean and bright, for the*
> *fine linen is the righteous acts of the saints.*
> *9 Then he said to me, "Write: 'Blessed are those who are called to the marriage*
> *supper of the Lamb!' " And he said to me,*
> *"These are the true sayings of God."*
> *10 And I fell at his feet to worship him. But he said to me,*
> *"See that you do not do that! I am your fellow servant,*
> *and of your brethren who have the testimony of Jesus.*
> *Worship God! For the testimony of Jesus is the spirit of prophecy."*

One of the most powerful ways that you can fight the enemy is with a prophetic word. Many times prophetic words come in our worship. When you are singing and glorifying him, you're using our voice to invite God into your battle. We were told by Jesus to pray God's will on earth as it is in heaven. In this portion of Scripture from the Book of Revelation, we see clearly that there is worship in heaven. When we all get to heaven at the marriage supper of the Lamb, we're going to be singing and worshiping him and testifying of his goodness and how he fought our battles for us. Heaven sounds like an exciting place. I enjoy telling stories and recounting God's goodness. Heaven sounds like a wonderful place. I love worship and praise. From a biblical perspective it looks like my life has been a gigantic rehearsal for mighty eternal reality.

> *Revelation 19:12-16*
> *12 His eyes were like a flame of fire, and on His head were many crowns. He had a name written that no one knew except Himself.*
> *13 He was clothed with a robe dipped in blood, and His name is called The Word of God.*
> *14 And the armies in heaven, clothed in fine linen, white and clean, followed Him on white horses.*
> *15 Now out of His mouth goes a sharp sword, that with it He should strike the nations. And He Himself will rule them with a rod of iron. He Himself treads the winepress of the fierceness and wrath of Almighty God.*
> *16 And He has on His robe and on His thigh a name written: KING OF KINGS AND LORD OF LORDS.*

Jesus's weapon here is the spoken word of God that comes out of His mouth. When He speaks, it strikes the nations. For He is the King of kings and the Lord of lords; He is the word of God. When we sing and we worship with lyrics that are the inspired by the word of God, it's a weapon against darkness. It saddens me when I see modern praise and worship leaders compromise and try to come up with some pseudo-spiritual sounding line or lyric. They are really not interested in pleasing God; they're interested in pleasing a producer or pseudo-spiritual audience.

We are to sing the word of God and to declare the word of God. We're saying his written word, and there's power in it. Don't worry about writing some appealing new lyric or line. Sing the inspired word of God and watch the power of God and the presence of God manifest in your services.

> *Ephesians 5:15-21*
> *15 See then that you walk circumspectly, not as fools but as wise,*
> *16 redeeming the time, because the days are evil.*
> *17 Therefore do not be unwise, but understand what the will of the Lord is.*
> *18 And do not be drunk with wine, in which is dissipation;*
> *but be filled with the Spirit,*
> *19 speaking to one another in psalms and hymns and spiritual songs, singing and making melody in your heart to the Lord,*
> *20 giving thanks always for all things to God the Father in the name of our Lord Jesus Christ,*
> *21 submitting to one another in the fear of God.*

The presence of God is supposed to be so satisfying that nothing else makes us happy. We are to be so filled up with the presence of God that it's the most satisfying thing in our life. Where are we to find our satisfaction and our fulfillment? In the presence of God. I've seen what alcoholism and addiction can do to people. Alcohol destroys lives. But when you've experienced the tangible, manifested presence of God, there is nothing more satisfying or more fulfilling. It's actually the greatest addiction. It's an addiction that will not harm you. It's an addiction that will not destroy your body. It's an addiction that will not make a fool out of you. It will become the most fulfilling thing you could ever do.

> *1 Thessalonians 5:16-22*
> *16 Rejoice always,*
> *17 pray without ceasing,*
> *18 in everything give thanks; for this is the will of God in Christ Jesus for you.*
> *19 Do not quench the Spirit.*
> *20 Do not despise prophecies.*
> *21 Test all things; hold fast what is good.*
> *22 Abstain from every form of evil.*

How you live your life is a witness. You can do things that will cause other people to fall into sin. Be careful what you do. But there are things in your life that can quench the anointing. And so it's important that if you have an anointing from God as a worship leader that you are to hold on to that and to guard that anointing on your life. You are to be filled with the presence of God, not with some artificial substance that's only going to hurt you in the long run. God wants you to be satisfied with Him. He wants to be more than enough. He wants you to sing and play and worship him and find your deepest satisfaction in His presence.

> *Romans 8:28*
> *[28] And we know that all things work together for good to those who love God, to those who are the called according to His purpose.*
>
> *Psalm 50:23*
> *[23] whoever offers praise glorifies Me; And to him who orders his conduct aright I will show the salvation of God."*

CHAPTER 8

The Anointing

*"God doesn't give us a mantle for yourself but for others, God gives you
the degree of a mantle to the degree that you give it away."*
~Ray Hughes, Selah Ministries

Let me be very clear: performing is not the same as being anointed.
Performance is about using one's own abilities and talents for the
sake of entertainment and self-promotion. Being anointed is entirely different. So let's break it down.

Unless you understand the anointing, another book on praise and worship is pointless. Every person is given a grace gift, a special skill that
comes from God. It is a natural ability or grace gifting that you have that
is personal to you. Everyone has a certain grace or gifting to do whatever
it is that they're called to do.

But it's different when you're talking about a minister of the gospel.
The ministry isn't really about the minister. Ministry is all about helping
others. When you take your natural ability and consecrate it to God, He
will move through you to help others. The anointing is separate from your
grace gift. God will take the gift of God or the talent that you develop,
and then when your heart is in the right place, the anointing falls and you
begin to see the supernatural operate in your gifting.

Before I came to Christ, I absolutely loved performing on stage. My mom and I were buddies, and we did a lot of performing together when I was young. My church put together the musical *Godspell* when I was in high school, which was my first introduction to the Gospel of Jesus Christ. I knew I could sing and I felt God's presence when I did. Later on in high school, I had the honor of landing the leading roles in my high school musicals. I sang and danced in the local community theater productions of *Sound of Music, The King and I, The Apartment,* and *Mouse Trap.*

When I was 16, I was able to perform in collegiate-level summer stock productions. I had talent. I knew it, and doors were opening for me at a very young age. I sang for television commercials and did some commercials up in Minneapolis. I worked hard and applied myself in every production. It was there that I learned a lot about technique, vocal training, how to handle myself on a stage, and how to sell a song. It was exciting and rewarding.

In college at the University of Northern Iowa, I studied musical theater dance and acting. I was starring in light Opera productions. It seemed like the future was bright for me. But it was empty. I wanted more.

The Holy Spirit had always been trying to get my attention, but in those young, ambitious years I didn't pay much attention to God. Looking back at it now, even in my loneliness God was doing what he could to get my attention. I remember the Holy Spirit prompting me to attend mass before heading down to the Hill in Cedar Falls. I also remember one winter morning walking to the Campus Crusade for Christ office but for some reason turning around before they answered the door. College had its ups and downs, but through the entire process I can say I was hungry for God.

Life changed drastically when I finally gave my life to Christ. I began to study the spirit and how the supernatural worked. I knew intuitively that the supernatural operated through music, but I didn't connect the concepts until I studied the anointing. I understand what it is to be a talented musician, but talent is not anointing. Spiritual things are spiritually discerned (1 Cor. 2:14). I've had hundreds of kids walk in my classroom and audition to lead worship. I have listened to incredibly talented kids with no anointing. On the other hand, I've had kids walk in my classroom who have little or no skill at all, but the anointing of God is all over them. The presence of God on someone's music starts with hard work and skill, but when the presence of God begins to move through that musician, you can feel the anointing.

What is the anointing?

Anointing has its origins in ancient shepherding, and it has significance for us today. Shepherds knew that if insects got into the sheep's wool and burrowed into the animal's head and ears, it could kill the sheep. To combat this situation, shepherds learned to pour oil on the sheep's wool, causing the insects to slide off the wool because it became too slippery for them to hold on.[6] The oil became a deterrent against the sheep's enemy. Similarly, when a minister of God flows in the anointing, it can absolutely combat spiritual enemies that were sent to destroy the saints of God. It is powerful!

The anointing of God is not to glorify the musician but to glorify God. The purpose of the anointing is to build the kingdom of God and set free those who are captive. Even Jesus had to have the anointing in order to do the ministry that God had called him to do. God anointed Jesus after he was baptized by John the Baptist in the Jordan River. Up until that time, Jesus hadn't done any miracles.

> *When He had been baptized, Jesus came up immediately from the water; and behold, the heavens were opened to Him, and He saw the Spirit of God descending like a dove and alighting upon Him.*
>
> *Matthew 3:16*

When you're under an anointing, you can feel it. You also know when it lifts. How you do know it? Trust me, you do. Because of the anointing, Jesus "went about doing good and healing all who were oppressed by the devil, for God was with Him" (Acts 10:38). *"For God was with him."* And

---

[6]"What is the Anointing?" https://www.gotquestions.org/anointed.html. Retrieved 12 March 2018.

God did the miraculous through him. He was fully God but he was fully man.

The anointing will be given to you when you need it at every phase in your ministry, and it will grow as you obey Him. It will help you and give you strength and wisdom. If you want the anointing to grow and get stronger, then you must obey. Jesus is our example. Philippians 2:8 says that "He humbled Himself and became obedient to the point of death, even the death of the cross." Think about it: It was this humility and act of obedience that brought about the greatest glory mankind has ever known.

Jesus told his disciples that they were not to go anywhere or do anything until they had received the baptism of the Holy Spirit. They were to wait in Jerusalem until they were endued with power from on high, and then when the power came upon them, they would be sent forth to fulfill their calling (Luke 24:49). Jesus was the Son of God the entire time He was here on earth. He came from heaven to earth to die for us and for our sins, but the anointing that he would need to fulfill what he had to do for you and me didn't come until He was baptized. Then the public ministry started.

You see, the power of God comes on you when you receive the Holy Spirit. That infilling changes everything. All of a sudden you don't have to do everything in your own strength but you have God's supernatural strength working through you. That power is what you depend on and it carries you.

Ultimately, the whole purpose of the anointing of God is to enable a man or woman of God to be a witness of Jesus Christ. Acts 1:8 says that "you shall receive power when the Holy Spirit has come upon you; and you shall be witnesses of Me…" The anointing of God never glorifies man; it always points to Jesus Christ. When you first give your life to Christ and you become a Christian, the Holy Spirit comes in you. And that's a beautiful born-again experience. But there is another experience that comes later. When you are baptized with the Holy Spirit with evidence of speaking in other tongues, this infilling with power will enable you to be a witness for Jesus Christ. The anointing dwells within you. And when you sing and you minister to others, the anointing inside of you is released through your singing voice or your musical instrument. The Holy Spirit is from God. He receives you and He enables you to do what you're called to do.

Anointing through the Ministry Gifts

God's anointing works in unique ways with the various callings He has for different people. The first group of people He anoints is the five-fold ministry gifts found in the book of Ephesians 4:11 – apostles, prophets, evangelists, pastors and teachers. God gives these gifts to the body of Christ to fulfill the ministry. Each one of these ministry offices has a different purpose or anointing. Even though the anointing is ultimately for the purpose of building the kingdom, each one operates in the anointing differently.

The Apostle is a sent one. He goes out and at times operates in all five ministry gifts. He is the powerhouse. He builds churches and establishes works. He is the overseer.

The Prophet pulls people into place and purpose. The Prophet operates in the vocal gifts to confirm the offices in the local church. They build up and edify the local church. They have a grace to pray and often work closely with worship leaders. They know when God is moving and when He is not.

The Evangelist is called to win the lost. Signs and wonders follow that office gift.

The Pastor is the shepherd who cares for the sheep and protects the people of God from false teachers. He works closely with the body of Christ and raises up believers.

The Teacher is the corrector of doctrine and helps establish the theology of the local church.

There are other special anointings in the gifts of the Spirit listed in First Corinthians 12:7-12, 27-31: word of wisdom, word of knowledge, faith, gifts of healings, working of miracles, prophecy, discerning of spirits, different kinds of tongues, interpretation of tongues, helps, and administrations. These gifts are incredibly important because they enable God's will to be accomplished in our lives. The gifts of the spirit are given to each member of the body of Christ. And on our journey with Christ, we learn what gifts we have been given.

When it comes to ministers of music, I see many of these gifts. Probably the most important ones are prophecy, administration and faith. Most of the time, ministers of music have a prophetic gifting not just for music but also prayer. The ministry of intercessory prayer and worship go hand in hand. You must know the mind of Christ before you pull worship sets. Ministers of music also operate in the area of helps and administration. Running a music department takes a lot of work. I mean, a lot of work!

Not only are we to be empowered with these gifts, but Paul tells us to "earnestly desire the best gifts" (1 Cor. 12:31). We are to desire to be used by God especially in the area of the prophetic. As ministers of music, we always want to know what the will of God is for the service. How do we know what to play or when to play it, and what does the Holy Spirit want to hear? It's also important to know that you have to be called by God to operate in these five-fold gifts. I often say, if you call yourself to an office, you have to anoint yourself. If you're truly called of God to operate in a five-fold ministry gift, you will be given the grace and the strength to do so. Trying to operate in an office gift you're not called to can harm the body of Christ and also harm the minister. You don't ever want to put yourself in a ministry office and give yourself the title without knowing that God has called you to operate in that gifting.

We are all called by God to operate in the gifts of the Spirit. However, the Lord will grant special anointings to certain individuals who seem to operate in higher degrees or levels of gifting. These gifts are operated in by faith. But to a certain extent they operate because someone is called into a specific ministry office. Every single one of us is called to some degree to the ministry of helps. If you've been in the ministry for any period of time, you know that ministry is hard work. It takes a group of hard-working servants with a team mentality to pull off successful ministry. The gifts of administration are extremely important. And these administrative gifts and roles in the local body are being trained to fully walk in a five-fold ministry gifts down the road. For you have an anointing from the holy one (1 John 2:20), and that anointing abides in you and remains in you.

For the Bible tells us that we are children of God and we have overcome the evil one because greater is he that is in us than he that is in the world (1 John 4:4). The gifting in you will be trained for purpose while you work in the local church. He will deal with your character, teaching you humility and faithfulness. He will teach you to submit to authority. These lessons are priceless and will equip you in the future for the fullness of your calling. Don't ever underestimate those years of service. They are so important. God wants to deal with your character before he puts you on a platform.

You have an anointing within you to enable you to overcome the world and to serve successfully in the body of Christ. The anointing is not something that is placed in us for some unknown reason, but it abides in us or it takes up its home inside our heart. It remains in us and it never leaves us.

The purpose of the anointing is to give us power. And that power is to confirm that Jesus is Lord. The power of God will never glorify us but will always glorify Jesus. Any miracles or signs and wonders that we walk in will point to the cross and the blood that was shed on the cross for our sins. The moment a minister of music begins to take credit for the power of God that flows through his instrument, he is in trouble. But God is great in us and we have the ability to overcome darkness and sin because greater is he that is in us than he who is in the world (John 4:4). We are to be a witness to the saving power of Jesus Christ, and we have the ability through Him to overcome the things that are in the world. The anointing does not make us famous or make us money or guarantee us the latest recording contract or movie deal. No, the anointing on our lives is there to glorify Jesus Christ.

God not only empowers you to walk out the call of God, but according to Scripture He comes to comfort you when you desperately need it. And let me tell you, at times in ministry you're going to have to be comforted by God himself. Ministry is stressful and can be heartbreaking. You will get your heart broken by people, but He will never let you down. He will sustain you and give you strength even when you feel rejected and abandoned. Those seasons can be so painful, but in the middle of those hard times you learn to depend on him ONLY. You can never look to man but to God. God promises in His Word according to Hebrews 13 that He will never leave us or forsake us. He will always walk us through difficult situations, and He will always be in us. Hard lessons are learned the hard way. But keep going. The best is yet to come.

When the apostles were waiting to go forth in ministry, they had to wait on the Holy Spirit in Jerusalem in the upper room. They had to wait on God until it was time to go forward. We will have the supernatural ability to endure and overcome difficulty. He is our comforter and he will enable us to walk through all kinds of difficult things. The more that we learn to trust God and to lean on the anointing, the more likely that that anointing that dwells within us will enable us to achieve what He's called us to do. The more dependent we are on God, the more the anointing will operate in our lives and enable us to fulfill the call of God on our lives. It will take perpetual infilling of the Holy Spirit. Oh, yes, we're filled with the Holy Spirit when we are baptized in the Holy Spirit, but when we praise and worship, sing, and pray, this process refreshes our spirit man or fills us up once again. You are literally charging your spirit man with power. I always tell my students, "You don't hesitate to charge your cell phone. Why don't you charge your spirit man so that you can walk out this calling with God?" You're going to have to renew your mind and wait on him to get that fresh anointing. We are to be continually filled with the spirit.

There is a greater anointing that is given to musicians that lead praise and worship. As worship leaders, it's important to understand this anointing that comes on us for the body of Christ. There were times in my life I felt His presence when I sang secular songs. I remember vividly singing the role of Mollie in the *Pirates of Penzance*. I was alone in the spotlight, and I could feel the presence of God on me. Years before that production, I was in rehearsals for *Sound of Music* and the Mother Abbess was telling my character Maria to trust God and go back to the Von Trapp family. I broke in rehearsals. God was all over me and I could feel it. My best friend Dana was the nun, the Mother Abbess, and she looked at me and wondered what I was crying about. I know now that in that moment the Holy Spirit was dealing with me about my calling and my life. I was so clueless. Thankfully, God kept working on me. But He was dealing with me about my calling and what I was going to do with my life. It's not like what I feel now when I am singing in the spirit or leading worship. When I lift my voice now, it's for Him.

In the Book of Acts, it is recorded that on the day of Pentecost after Jesus' resurrection, the disciples were all gathered together and began to speak in tongues and worship (Acts 2:1). It says, "they were in one accord." It's so important for the body of Christ to get together on a weekly basis and to worship. I enjoy listening to teachers and preachers on YouTube or listening to podcasts or watching Christian television. All of these media outlets have much to offer you as you grow in the Lord. Christian media is important and it can teach and train you about the things of God in ministry. There's nothing wrong with any of these things. But the Bible clearly says that we are to meet with other believers so that we can receive the word of God and to build each other up in our faith.

As Solomon's Temple was dedicated to the Lord, the presence of God came so strongly on the musicians and singers that a cloud of glory filled the house of God (2 Chron. 5:13-14). When God's presence comes, the Shekinah glory presence of God can be seen. I've never seen in the spirit realm, but I have seen Shekinah glory in praise and worship services. It looks like a mist hanging over the people. It's a beautiful thing. These manifestations happen when the body of Christ is in agreement and when there's unity in our prayer and worship. When we as worship leaders have led the people to a place where everyone is in agreement, there's nothing stopping the flow of the presence of God. That's when we experience something called the corporate anointing.

Corporate Anointing

The corporate anointing is what happens when the believers all come together in one place and they have one purpose to lift up the name of Jesus. This is a little bit different than an individual anointing. The corporate anointing will bring a heavier presence. When there is a strong corporate anointing, that's when you see miracles, signs, and wonders. That's the beauty of being a praise and worship leader. We sing and worship, and our music brings people together in unity. And it's this unity that the glory of God can move or fill a place.

When Grant and I moved to Tulsa in the '90s, we would attend Rhema Bible Training Center meetings. The Rhema Singers and Band sang and led worship for the renowned faith teacher Kenneth Hagin. Ministers from all over the world would come to Broken Arrow for these meetings because they were hungry to experience the presence of the Lord. They knew if the Holy Spirit fell and there was a corporate anointing on the worship, God would speak. That's where I learned what the corporate anointing looked like and how it felt. There was so much unity in these meetings. These ministers understood how to praise and worship and how to focus on God, and we saw some powerful manifestations of the Spirit of God in that place.

Our job as ministers of music is to bring unity among the people that are attending our services. When we sing and glorify God together, something supernatural happens. The power of God falls and people begin to be changed by the presence of God. God longs to move among His people, and He loves to move when there is agreement.

This also can happen in small groups or in small prayer meetings. I saw it all the time in   my classroom among my praise and worship leaders. When Paul and Silas were in jail, they sang and worshiped and the foundations of the prison were shaken. Even though they were a small group worshiping Jesus together, God still moved mightily through them. Don't ever despise the days of small beginnings. Some of the greatest worship leaders I know leading the body of Christ today started out in small groups or at home cell groups. They led worship in Bible studies and in prayer groups, learning how to flow and how to minister to the Lord. Over time, God began to open doors for them because of their faithfulness and because of their hearts for him. There's also something that happens to the musician's skill level when he has to play regularly for people. The discipline of preparing sets and learning to flow in a small group is what will enable them down the road to lead successfully in front of large groups. This process can often take a while. But don't get frustrated because over time if you're faithful and you work hard, God will reward you. He will open doors for you. It's also important that you learn how to work with other people. When you work with a praise and worship band, you have to learn how to serve each other, which is a process as well. Learning to work with others and their different personalities is very important when you're in ministry.

No matter who you are or how big you get in the ministry (especially in the ministry of music), you must have a pastor. If you have a pastor who you have a relationship with and you can be discipled. You grow in Christ. You won't get sucked into sin or be deceived by the enemy. When you're called of God to be a minister of music, there is a different level of warfare than other callings. When you have the ability to open heaven and to usher in a corporate anointing, you are a powerful weapon in the kingdom of God. The enemy would like to knock you out before you ever get started. I'm convinced that's why there is such warfare over young musicians. It's because they are such a threat to the kingdom of darkness. For you were built by God for such a time as this. You have taken your talent, consecrated it, waited on the Lord until it was time, served the people diligently in those training years, and then, when it's time to go forward, God is going to use you in a mighty way, and the glory of God will follow you and your ministry. That's the process He uses, and that's when you will see the glory of God fill the house.

Guard the Anointing

There's an old saying in ministry that there are three things that can cause a minister to fall: the girls, the gold, or the glory. In other words, the enemy will use different things to get you to sin. Women are drawn to men that carry the anointing. They see a man on the platform that appears to be perfect. Unstable women can be drawn to that. Many ministers of music fall into adultery and their ministries or destroyed. Paul reminded the Corinthians, "Flee sexual immorality" because "your body is the temple of the Holy Spirit" (1 Cor. 6:18,19). And I'm reminding you of the same thing. If you have an issue in this area, confide in a church leader who can keep you accountable. Your ministry is worth it.

Other worship leaders become greedy. They misuse funds and take advantage of those that are giving into their ministries and they fall as well. Greed can make a person want to compromise their character or morals for the sake of more worldly gain. We're not to love money or anything more than we love God Himself. Keep your eyes on the goal of glorifying Him, and He will ensure that you have what you need. Continue to tithe, give to the poor, stay generous, and seek the kingdom of God first, "then all these things will be added to you" (Matt. 6:33). He owns it all, and He is a good Father who knows how to provide for us.

God will not share His glory with anyone. The glory of God is for Him alone. Don't ever let the enemy deceive you. I know what it's like to sing and to worship and have the power of God flow out of me. There's no greater feeling in the world. When that power flows out of me, it is because of God inside of me. The presence of God in me doesn't glorify me, but it glorifies my maker. As long as we stay humble and broken and we give the glory to Him, then we know that He will continue to use us. We can sing and worship and watch the glory of God fall. When we release His presence through our instruments and our talents, the anointing can fall and we can see the miraculous.

Don't settle for entertainment. Don't settle for talent. Seek God, stay humble and stay broken before him. Don't allow your ego to destroy you. Take the gifting that God has given you and use it for Him and for the kingdom, and you will experience the most remarkable life. You were born to see more. You were born to lead revival. Now is the time. Now more than ever we don't need entertainment on the church platform. We must experience His presence under the anointing of worship leaders who love

Him and are broken for His service. He uses those whose hearts are right before Him. Give Him your talent and He will give you many others.

We are at an important time in church history where God is raising up champion worship leaders for him and for the kingdom. There are worship leaders all over the world who want to run their race and they want to win it! I remember watching the movie, *Secretariat,* about a horse that won the Triple Crown in the 1970s. Secretariat was a beautiful horse, but he had an unusually large heart. His heart was his gift, and he could run easily because God built him that way. I love the movie scene where the horse just took off and ran with everything in him to win the final race. It always makes me cry. He was born to run. It was his gifting.

You are born to run with the anointing of God on your worship.

It is your gifting.

Run hard… God is with you.

Consecration

When I first got born again, one of the spiritual concepts I didn't understand was consecration. I was raised in a good home with good parents, but we definitely didn't think about ministry. My mom sang every Sunday in church. She loved God and sang for God. She knew she had a gift from God, but she never thought about it being a ministry unto the Lord. My grandmother Bernadine was a great singer who also loved the Lord. But I don't think they studied the priesthood. Unless we are taught, we don't understand that music is holy.

God wanted all of my gifting and talent. However, I had no idea about worship either. Then I surrendered my life to Christ and began to study the ministry of music.

When I was filled with the Holy Spirit, everything in my life began to change. It was a long process. I had to re-evaluate my values and priorities. I knew God wanted to do something supernatural with me, but all I could think about was fame and fortune. That's how most musicians find success. But success in the kingdom of God is a very different thing. To be truly successful, God wants everything. He wants all of you. He wants all of your gift. Scripture says that He is a jealous God and that He loves us with an everlasting love. He desires to be with us, and His presence comes in our praises.

Guarding my gifting didn't make any sense to me. This means is I am careful what I do and what I listen to, and I protect the presence of God on my life and in my music. I had grown up in an environment where I had to promote myself in order to get noticed. Self-promotion is what you do to make it in the entertainment industry. It takes a strong sense of self in order to go anywhere. When I truly surrendered my life to Christ, a lot of that had to be broken in me. I had to allow him to do something deep in my heart in order to submit to the call of God on my life. And I had to be willing to be different and I had to be comfortable with it.

I must admit all of my life I've struggled with wanting acceptance from others. I especially struggle with this when I go back home amongst friends. Everyone likes to talk about what they've done with their life. I love the people that I went to school with. However, over the years, I've become acutely aware of what I'm going to take into eternity with me. I started living with an eternity mindset. My goal is to take people to heaven with me. Things, positions, and careers don't mean as much to me. I am thankful I decided to sell out and give my life to Christ.

Leviticus 8:31-36

31 And Moses said to Aaron and his sons, "Boil the flesh at the door of the tabernacle of meeting, and eat it there with the bread that is in the basket of consecration offerings, as I commanded, saying, 'Aaron and his sons shall eat it.'

32 What remains of the flesh and of the bread you shall burn with fire.

33 And you shall not go outside the door of the tabernacle of meeting for seven days, until the days of your consecration are ended. For seven days he shall consecrate you.

34 As he has done this day, so the LORD has commanded to do, to make atonement for you. 35 Therefore you shall stay at the door of the tabernacle of meeting day and night for seven days, and keep the charge of the LORD, so that you may not die; for so I have been commanded."

36 So Aaron and his sons did all the things that the LORD had commanded by the hand of Moses.

In this portion of Scripture, the Levites were set aside for ministry. They had to go through a season of dedicating themselves to the Lord. It was called "the days of your consecration." The Lord has a process he takes all musicians through. There's going to be a season in time when He will ask you to consecrate your gift and consecrate your life. When he does, it will be a holy thing.

> *Leviticus 8:22-24*
> *22 And he brought the second ram, the ram of consecration. Then Aaron and his sons laid their hands on the head of the ram,*
> *23 and Moses killed it. Also he took some of its blood and put it on the tip of Aaron's right ear, on the thumb of his right hand, and on the big toe of his right foot.*
> *24 Then he brought Aaron's sons. And Moses put some of the blood on the tips of their right ears, on the thumbs of their right hands, and on the big toes of their right feet. And Moses sprinkled the blood all around on the altar.*

Moses took the blood of the sacrifice and he put it on the ear and upon the thumb of his right hand and on the great toe of his right foot. Hands and toes and ears are all important for musicians. These appendages enable us to play for God and the blood of Jesus is to be applied to our ears, hands, and feet. The blood is applied to where we go and where we stand. When we minister, the blood is applied to our ears and what we hear. We are to guard what we listen to. We are to guard our heart and guard our gift for the ministry.

> *Exodus 29:29-32*
> *29 "And the holy garments of Aaron shall be his sons' after him, to be anointed in them and to be consecrated in them.*
> *30 That son who becomes priest in his place shall put them on for seven days, when he enters the tabernacle of meeting to minister in the [a] holy place.*
> *31 "And you shall take the ram of the consecration and boil its flesh in the holy place. 32 Then Aaron and his sons shall eat the flesh of the ram, and the bread that is in the basket, by the door of the tabernacle of meeting.*

Again, there is a blood sacrifice and it was offered in the holy place. For Aaron was to set aside men of God and consecrate them for ministry.

> *Exodus 28:3*
> *³ So you shall speak to all who are gifted artisans, whom I have filled with the spirit of wisdom, that they may make Aaron's garments, to consecrate him, that he may minister to Me as priest.*

In Exodus 28, it says we are to consecrate ourselves so that we can minister of God. We minister to Him and we please Him. We set aside our music and our instruments for Him so that we can glorify Him.

> *2 Chronicles 26:18-19*
> *¹⁸ And they withstood King Uzziah, and said to him, "It is not for you, Uzziah, to burn incense to the LORD, but for the priests, the sons of Aaron, who are consecrated to burn incense. Get out of the sanctuary, for you have trespassed! You shall have no honor from the LORD God."*
> *¹⁹ Then Uzziah became furious; and he had a censer in his hand to burn incense. And while he was angry with the priests, leprosy broke out on his forehead, before the priests in the house of the LORD, beside the incense altar.*

There are other times in Scripture where men did not take holy things seriously. They were told to get out of the sanctuary quickly because they had no honor before the Lord. The Lord became furious with them. I'm so thankful that I live in the new covenant. I am not under the law, I have a new covenant relationship with God. It's hard to think of God being displeased by disobedience. The holy things are not to be played with.

> *Psalm 4:3*
> *³ But know that the LORD has set apart for Himself him who is godly; The LORD will hear when I call to Him.*

There are great rewards for setting yourself aside for ministry. When you consecrate your heart, you consecrate your life. God can use you. And he promises you that God will hear you when you call.

> *Romans 12:1-2*
> *¹ I beseech you therefore, brethren, by the mercies of God, that you present your bodies a living sacrifice, holy, acceptable to God, which is your reasonable service.*
> *² And do not be conformed to this world, but be transformed by the renewing of*

your mind, that you may prove what is that good and acceptable and perfect will of God.

Our very lives are sacrifices unto Him. When you present your entire self to Him and you make it holy unto Him, you're not going to look or act like the world. You're going to be different. I have no problem with musicians wanting to be skillful. There's a time to study. We can learn a lot about skillfulness in secular environments. But it's a very different thing when you're talking about ministry. If you want to see the power of God manifest in your music, it's going to take sacrifice. And when you're transformed and your mind has become renewed, you will see God move.

Proverbs 23:26
26 My son, give me your heart, And let your eyes observe my ways.

We live in a difficult world now. It's very hard to be a Christian and to guard what you see. You can try to protect your eyes and you can try to protect your heart, but inevitably you're going to see and watch things that are going to be hard to erase. Renewing your mind, guarding your eyes and then asking God to cleanse you and to keep you clean before him will enable you to minister effectively for him.

We're called to be vessels of honor. We are called to be ministers unto the Lord.

2 Timothy 2:21-26
21 Therefore if anyone cleanses himself from the latter, he will be a vessel for honor, sanctified and useful for the Master, prepared for every good work.
22 Flee also youthful lusts; but pursue righteousness, faith, love, peace with those who call on the Lord out of a pure heart.
23 But avoid foolish and ignorant disputes, knowing that they generate strife.
24 And a servant of the Lord must not quarrel but be gentle to all, able to teach, patient,
25 in humility correcting those who are in opposition, if God perhaps will grant them repentance, so that they may know the truth,
26 and that they may come to their senses and escape the snare of the devil, having been taken captive by him to do his will.

1 Thessalonians 5:23-24
23 Now may the God of peace Himself sanctify you completely; and may your whole spirit, soul, and body be preserved blameless at the coming of our Lord Jesus Christ.
24 He who calls you is faithful, who also will do it.

2 Kings 23:1-3
1 Now the king sent them to gather all the elders of Judah and Jerusalem to him.
2 The king went up to the house of the LORD with all the men of Judah, and with him all the inhabitants of Jerusalem--the priests and the prophets and all the people, both small and great. And he read in their hearing all the words of the Book of the Covenant which had been found in the house of the LORD.
3 Then the king stood by a pillar and made a covenant before the LORD, to follow the LORD and to keep His commandments and His testimonies and His statutes, with all his heart and all his soul, to perform the words of this covenant that were written in this book. And all the people took a stand for the covenant.

I love King Josiah. I can remember as a young Christian reading the story about this young king who decided he was going to take a stance against idolatry in Israel. He was brave and courageous. Josiah was more courageous than the leadership at the time. This young man took a bold stance. He decided it was time to clean the house. He was going to clean up all of the idol worship. Josiah inspires me. This portion of Scripture still impresses me. It's one of the reasons I named my son Josiah. Josiah means "the fire of God" – fire that would come in and burn out all of the things are not of God. The fire of God will burn the world out of you. The fire of God will eliminate the impurities in your heart. The fire of God will cleanse you.

Gold is weighty. But in order to get pure gold, you have to get all of the impurities out of it. All of the impurities have to be heated up and they rise to the surface and then those impurities can be skimmed off the very top. What is left is something of great worth and great value. When you allow the fire of God to go into your heart, there are things that are there that he will begin to clean out. There are things that will begin to burn; he will begin to eliminate things in you and in your heart. It's a beautiful process. Don't resist it. Allow him to go in there and to burn those things that are not of him. Don't resist the heat. Allow those things to rise to the surface so they can be dealt with. And when you go through this process over and over again – when you allow God to clean you out – what will be left is a musician that carries substance and has great worth and value in the kingdom. Decide to be that vessel! The reward is great!

The Church knew what the psalmist knew: Music praises God. Music is well or better able to praise him than the building of the church and all its decoration; it is the Church's greatest ornament.

~Igor Stravinsky

CHAPTER 9

Planning a Worship
or Chapel Service

*"The aim and final end of all music should be none other than
the glory of God and the refreshment of the soul."*
~Johann Sebastian Bach

*"Success doesn't have anything to do with the outcome,
it's all in the process"*
Steffany Gretzinger ,Bethel Worship

P lanning, preparing, and coaching a good worship set takes time and prayer. Understanding why you are doing it gives the set meaning and purpose. If you don't look at all aspects of worship leading, you can get in a boring cycle and it can be a religious ritual that's dry and empty of the presence of God.

This is especially true at a private Christian school where students and teachers can take chapels for granted over time. There is a tendency to come to chapels because it's required and not even expect God's spirit to move. That's why it's important to go back and review why we do what we do. What are the biblical reasons for leading people into the presence of God? Why do we have worship at the beginning of the service? Is it just a way to corral students together and control them so we can get them to settle down to focus on the Word?

Some churches treat worship as the entertainment that draws a crowd so that the message can be heard. I disagree with that. If you go back to the biblical mandate set in scripture, we can see why we worship God. We worship Him the way we do because His Word instructs us to do it. We don't do it out of habit or routine. It's holy before Him, and it's His priority and His idea. He wants to be worshiped and glorified. And He wants us to do it from our hearts and not because we're forced to do it.

Encourage the Body of Believers

The primary focus of the church is to gather the believers together and to encourage and instruct the body on the Christian life. We are to exalt God. Exaltation is the believer's appropriate response to God. It's supposed to be the focus of the body of Christ, and that focus is to always be on Christ our savior and His sacrifice for us. Jesus is the head of the Church. The focus of exaltation is vertical. It's heaven word. It's where we relate and directly look to or point towards God. The first priority of the church is to worship God.

> *Jesus said to him, "'You shall love the LORD your God with all your heart, with all your soul, and with all your mind.'* [38] *This is the first and great commandment.*
>
> *Matthew 22:37, 38*

The world shows no favoritism – we're all being hit by one thing or another in life. Some show up to church absolutely exhausted by all that's happening around and to them. Everyone needs to be encouraged, strengthened, and lifted up. That's why when young people are learning to select praise and worship sets, it's so important that they seek the Lord. They need to pray and ask the Lord what He wants the people to sing and why.

A sensitive worship leader will hear what the Holy Spirit wants to sing and what the Holy Spirit wants to say in a service. Learning to hear is a process. Rookie worship leaders are going to pull good and bad sets and will learn from both. It's all part of the process of learning to lead, and its normal. What's wonderful is when the rookie worship leader pulls the perfect song in the right key and it lines up with what the speaker is saying at that moment. There's no greater reward. Why? The Holy Spirit has been able to move in a unique way to meet the needs of the people. The word edify is an important word. As believers we are to strengthen and encourage the body of believers. To edify the church and worship means to teach, encourage, equip and discipline for the purpose of building up or strengthening the local church.

Evangelize the Lost

There are certain things I'm kind of picky about when it comes to selecting worship sets. One of them is the lyrics of the song. What is the theme of the song? How does everything connect together in a set?

One of the primary purposes of worship is to evangelize the lost. Not everyone that comes to church or at Chapel service is born again. When people come to our services, they don't understand Christian church worship. All of that is taught over time to them by our teachers and in our services.

Worship is a form of evangelism because we are proclaiming the goodness of the gospel in the message and song. In singing the lyrics of the songs, people learn the theology of the church. Every song should line up theologically. Ultimately, our songs should encourage students to become worshipers of Christ. When we sing about His goodness and what He did on the cross for us, it points everyone to Jesus. So the ultimate purpose for the worship service is to bring together those that know him and those that don't-to glorify God through song. The lyrics will also establish the theology of the church.

The great hymns of all time tell of His greatness or what He has done for us. We don't sing songs about how poor and pathetic we are, but how great and glorious God is. We make musical decisions not to focus our attention on our problems but to exalt the answer to every problem – and that's Jesus and his gift of the Holy Spirit that dwells in us and gives us the ability to overcome in this life, ultimately giving us eternal life.

Practical Steps to Setting up a Worship Service

Each church has a different philosophy of worship, but that philosophy should be clear. It should be clearly communicated how long the worship should service should be, the focus of the worship, and even the style of worship. It's important that all of this is clearly communicated so that the leaders in the church can work closely with the band.

My situation was different because I was working with young worship leaders who only knew a few songs. Kids could only play in a few keys but we did the best we could at the skill level we were at. And when we gave what we could to God, He always multiplied it.

Most of the time our worship services were structured, but sometimes it's good to shake it up and do something different. Over time, worship services can become religious rituals. There's nothing wrong with varying the structure or the order of services. In fact, I think it helps at times to keep things a little bit unpredictable. If we don't vary things, we are really no different than the liturgical churches of the Catholic Church in the Middle Ages. The Catholic Church had a clear liturgy and a clear structure to follow. I came out of a structured, religious, Episcopalian background. I'm thankful for the Word that was in those services because it later became a foundation for my life. But when I became a born-again, spirit-filled Christian, I wanted to be in a worship service or setting where the Holy Spirit was allowed to move and the gifts of the Spirit operated and moved freely.

Now don't get me wrong: I appreciate all the modern technology available to worship leaders. Multitracks and Ableton loops can make worship leaders sound like professional musicians, even if they're not. And in this consumer-driven church environment, having professional sounding worship is important. But it should never limit the prophetic move of the

Holy Ghost in a service. To my knowledge, as of the writing of this book, the only technology that allows freedom and spontaneity in a worship song is Ableton. Ableton was designed for disc jockeys so that they could take portions of songs and connect them together live. Most of the time, every moment of the song is programmed in advance. And I don't have a problem with it as long as the band is able and is prepared for a spontaneous move of God musically. I guess I'm just kind of old school. Tracks for me are a little bit like lip-synching. It's good, but it's kind of fake. Musicians who have the skillful ability to run the software can make the songs sound like they should. The problem is Christians now have the ability to listen to professional worship all the time especially through Spotify or Pandora. That's great, but when you come to church, it's not going to sound like a professional Hillsong band. You just don't have all of the main stage sounds necessary. And, frankly, in the local church most churches don't have the budget to pay musicians that can play on that level of skillfulness. And if they are skillful, do they have the heart to worship God? Is this just a gig that they do on the side to make money, or are they really intent on ministering to the Lord? If at all possible, always stick with the rookie musicians who have the heart but not necessarily the skillfulness. Mentor them and allow them to grow because the heart is connected to you and to your work. They will over time get better and better.

Musicians have a tendency to have large egos and to need a lot of encouragement and support. When they grow and play in a loving, nurturing environment and they're willing to give their gift to God, God will multiply that gift just like in the parable of the talents (see Matthew 25). Don't bury your gifts; give them to God and let Him multiply them.

The issue here is if you have been given a talent, then you need to take that talent and give it to the Lord for His kingdom and for His service. He wants to take it and do more with it. I cannot tell you how many students I have had over the years who have had very limited ability, but they loved God. They took that limited ability and went to work. They decided that even if they didn't sound the best and if they weren't the most skillful, they would take what they had and give it to Him. Over time the gift just exploded in them. All of a sudden they were not just playing acoustic guitar, but they were playing bass and electric guitar. Eventually they decided they could figure out how to make chord shapes on the piano, and they were off and running. How about the kid who just wants to play guitar but has no desire or ability to sing? He is perfectly comfortable playing guitar where he is and decides he wants to stay there. But the Lord knows there is more there. If he will get over being self-conscious and just give that voice to Him, it will grow. Honestly, he needs a supportive, loving environment with other men who sing. I see this year after year. When men sing together, they grow vocally. It's so important for men to hear other men. When a man is listening to another man sing, he knows how it should sound and is willing to try to imitate that sound. It will affect how it feels in his head as well as how it feels in the mask (front of the face). When those feelings become normal, then the singing process and ability begin to explode. Suddenly they are hearing pitches in their head and they can match pitch. Singing is 99 percent hard work and 1 percent natural-born talent. Singing skills are not the easiest to develop, and in men it's even harder because of the change at puberty. Some men have very dramatic voice changes which can make them even more insecure about their speaking voice and singing voice. Getting over that change can be very difficult, and I have seen the voice drop a couple of times in puberty (Low Basses).

This entire process can be very difficult, but God still wants to use that voice. He wants to be glorified through that young man, and He knows that kid's heart. If that guy will just keep singing and keep developing the voice and working on the other musical skills, then over time it will grow. It's like a large puzzle. All of the pieces are there, but they must be developed over time and put into place. After a while, each skill or puzzle piece will begin to make the big picture. Each skill will get stronger and more stable. Each time you sing or play in front of others, confidence will grow, fear and performance anxiety will leave, and the gift will begin to grow. All things come together with time and experience.

My husband raises exotic birds. In our backyard we have a large aviary and an outdoor pen where the birds can fly and grow freely. My husband comes home from a long day at work and goes outside to tend to these gentle, little animals who love to sing. He loves to sit on our back porch and listen to them. The open aviary is right off our master bedroom, and when the sun rises we have a little praise and worship concert going on in our back yard. As soon as the sun breaks on the horizon, the birds begin to sing. It's a beautiful thing. We have doves from Australia. They are very small, but they have a beautiful song and they love to sing to each other. I love to talk about my crazy back yard in my classroom of young male vocalists. Here is why: The baby birds are born and quickly they want to start cooing, but they listen to and study the sounds made by the other males. While the older, more expert males begin to sing, they watch each other and study each other and then eventually imitate each other's songs. This is a lot of fun during mating season when every male we have is eagerly looking for a girlfriend. Needless to say, Grant and I have a lot of good laughs on the porch watching all of this fervent singing going on!

The bottom line is that men learn how to sing from other men and how to match that sound. All singers – male and female – need to learn basic breath control and mouth positions. Open vowels are so important. You must get all the sound out of the mouth and into the house or the microphone. The presence of God rides on the sound, and so the sound that you make with your body was designed to be heard. Your life is dependent on the air you breathe. You cannot live without the air you breathe. Well, the fact that you can breathe is another indicator that you were designed by God to worship and glorify him and that you need to sing. When you breathe in, you are breathing in His presence, and when you exhale, you are letting His presence out. It comes in your singing voice and in your preaching voice. God uses the foolish things to confound the wise (1 Cor. 1:27). He uses man's sound to touch His people, His creation.

Tempered worship leaders who have been around the block for a while will tell you things they don't like talking about publicly. When you try to minister out of your natural talent, you will fall on your face. You know... Remember the time you stood on the platform and suddenly forgot your words? The simple chord progression you were playing and you went blank? All of a sudden, your brain is gone and you can't remember anything? Well, it has happened to me and to many of my students. When you are humbled like that, you never approach the platform again with arrogance or pride. You go with great humility. You ask God to help you with every word and every note you play. Yes, you rehearse. Yes, you memorize your music and prepare, but you know that if the enemy can get in there and mess things up, he will. You have to take authority over distractions and spiritual harassment. You decide that you are not going to let that happen. You are going to stand on the platform humble, broken and desperate, knowing you can't do anything without Him. God will use and quickly promote the humble minister of music.

Most people think that worship just happens. Good musicians do everything they can to make the worship set look flawless. The transitions are perfect, and the keys are connected. The order of the set is clear, and you know God is going to move because the presence of God was so strong in rehearsals. When the Holy Spirit is moving in the rehearsal, you know God is going to do something different today. He is going to move.

I love it when we have a set ready to go and God shows up and moves totally differently. You can do that with seasoned and well-trained musicians who have a great ear and an understanding of the Nashville chord system, but with rookie kids who are learning, that's another thing. Rookie kids need options and extra songs to play just in case the speaker doesn't show or the glory falls and the altars are full of hurting people. Good worship leading takes hours and hours to learn. You can't learn about it in a book – you just have to do it. You have to get over your fear and intimidation and start with what you know and allow God to use you.

Pulling a Worship Set

Learning to pull a worship set is a process. The most important thing you can do is pray and then during the rehearsal process see what goes well and then try to figure out what the Holy Spirit is moving through during the rehearsal. When you first get started, pick songs that are simple and that you know very well so that you don't have to work hard while you are gaining experience. I have my kids listen to sets at youth at our church and see what songs fit together. Listen to other worship bands online and even read and see what others are pulling.

The main consideration is not the tempo but the heart posture. When you open a praise and worship set, it starts with praise first. Most praise songs are medium to fast tempo, and then as the worship service proceeds, then the more intimate songs that are slower in nature are next. Its doesn't always happen that way, but generally it does.

Start out with songs you LOVE. When you are alone with God, what do you love to sing to Him? Really, anything goes as long as its biblical and easy to follow. Make sure the keys are correct and that the lead vocalist can sing it easily. Remember, your goal when pulling a worship set is to get people singing so if it's in a very high or low key, no one can sing with you. You have to get the people singing. You can pull from some popular Christian songs, but many popular Christian songs are telling stories or encouraging others. There is nothing wrong with that, but when we pull songs for a praise and worship set, the songs are vertically directed. They point upwards towards God and to Heaven. Christian songs that encourage, inspire, or entertain are more horizontal in nature. They are things that can be sung over people or to encourage and uplift people, but they are not worship.

I love the song "I Can Only Imagine" by Mercy Me. It's about heaven. It's a fantastic song, but it won't always work in a worship set. I love to pull in older songs and even do a new arrangement of an old worship hymn. Hymns are great, and they tell the theology of the church. The really good ones are still being sung today and they can be so effective in a worship set. I love "Great is Thy Faithfulness" or "There is a Fountain Filled with Blood."

I think it's also important for all worship leaders to learn classical Christmas and Easter music. If you are going to lead worship in the local church, you going to have to know "Silent Night" and "Away in the Manger." Many effective worship leaders know how to take traditional Christian music and work it into a service.

I always have my students learn music for altar calls. They need to know Blood songs for healing and deliverance, Holy Spirit themed songs for altars where people come to receive the baptism of the Holy Spirit, and songs that inspire repentance. These songs need to be memorized and then the band should all know them in an easy key. Ladies, I recommend the key of D and for most men the key of G works well.

Worship leaders should always consult the pastor or the leader of the service they are playing for. If there is a question about a song, it's better to wait and show it to your pastor and discuss the song before you try to lead it on the platform. You are there to help the pastor serve the people, and it's important that you are in agreement with him. Don't ever use songs that the pastor disapproves of. If you do, you are in rebellion to authority. All worship leaders and helps ministry need to read John Bevere's book *Under Cover*. Pastors have to answer to God for what happens in their church, and a good pastor always thinks about and protects the sheep.

Secular songs are generally NOT about God or going to give God glory. My sister-in-law was at a church in North Carolina a few years back and they decided to play the old rock and roll song, "Stairway to Heaven," during communion. They accused her of being legalistic for objecting to them playing it in church. She told the pastor that during communion she is talking to God and repenting of her sin and the song was a distraction for her and it hindered her worship. The pastor told her she was legalistic and they were just doing everything they could to be relevant. What a stupid statement. There are so many wonderful songs out there that are modern and would enhance a person's worship experience. Music in the church should never draw someone away from God or cause them not to focus on the Lord. If it's a distraction, get rid of it. We serve God as worship leaders, and what we do matters for eternity.

CHAPTER 10

Eternal Worship

Your kingdom come.
Your will be done
On earth as it is in heaven.
~ Matthew 6:10

"We need to remember one thing and that is to sit at the feet of Jesus"
~Cory Asbury

It's hard to think of us as eternal beings. We get so busy with our everyday lives that we forget someday we're going to stand before God on Judgment Day. This reality hit me hard when my mother passed away in 2004. She was an amazing musician and a larger-than-life personality. She had an anointing on her singing. The presence of God would come on her so strongly when she sang. She knew it was her gift, and she was aware that God had given it to her. When she passed away, heaven became much more real to me, so I began to study about heaven.

Right about that time I came across Randy Alcorn's book, *Heaven.* That book changed me for the better. Eternal life became real. And I began to think of my praise and worship rehearsals more like a dress rehearsal for heaven. Think about it: we were created for praise and worship. When we step into eternity, we will be with Him forever and we will be worshiping Him. It's so vital that we remember that as we lead praise and worship. We live in a fame- and fortune-driven culture. We're surrounded by media that tries to tell us what's important and what's not. For some, the quest to become famous is so important. But what we should long for more than anything else is to be famous in heaven.

> *John 4:23-24*
> ²³ *But the hour is coming, and now is, when the true worshipers will worship the Father in spirit and truth; for the Father is seeking such to worship Him.* ²⁴ *God is Spirit, and those who worship Him must worship in spirit and truth."*

I'm not sure how most people picture God. I think many people think of God as some grumpy old man in the sky trying to ruin a good time. But biblically that just doesn't cut it. In fact, I was very surprised one day to find an amazing Scripture about God. I spent many years teaching kids how to sing. Singing doesn't come easily; it's a skill that is learned over time. So I just jumped for joy when I found this amazing Scripture:

> *Zephaniah 3:17*
> ¹⁷ *The LORD your God in your midst, The Mighty One, will save; He will rejoice over you with gladness, He will quiet you with His love, He will rejoice over you with singing."*

I never thought about God being a singer, but according to this Scripture not only does He sing but He *enjoys* singing. In fact, He rejoices over me with singing.

Angels and God's Plan for Worship

One of the most interesting studies I've ever done about eternal things was a study on angels done by Terry Law. Terry was the founder of Living Sound praise and worship band out of Oral Roberts University in the 70s. Terry wrote a fantastic book on praise and worship, but his book on angels is equally as amazing.

Angels were created by God. They have functions and purposes. Their primary function is to deliver messages. There are a few angels that are so important that their names are actually listed in Scripture. Michael is the archangel; he is a warring angel who looks over Israel. Gabriel is a leader of the angels, and he is involved in delivering messages. Lucifer was created in heaven specifically for praise and worship. He was the angel that guarded the throne room in heaven. He was an anointed angel. When the tabernacle was built, there were two angels that covered the mercy seat and guarded the Ark of the covenant. Lucifer was like that, only he did it in the throne room of heaven. He was the anointed cherub who led worship in heaven.

Ezekiel 28:14-15
14 "You were the anointed cherub who covers; I established you; You were on the holy mountain of God; You walked back and forth in the midst of fiery stones.
15 You were perfect in your ways from the day you were created,
Till iniquity was found in you.

It is interesting that the root word for the name *Lucifer* comes from "praise, to be bright or to shine, to be splendid, to celebrate, to glorify, and to be famous." It is a good indication that his primary function in heaven was praise and worship. The word is closely related to *hallelujah*. But Lucifer, aka Satan, became arrogant and desired to be worshiped, and that was eventually his downfall.

Isaiah 14:11-15
11 Your pomp is brought down to Sheol, And the sound of your stringed instruments;
The maggot is spread under you, And worms cover you.'
12 "How you are fallen from heaven, O Lucifer, son of the morning!
How you are cut down to the ground, You who weakened the nations!
13 For you have said in your heart: 'I will ascend into heaven,
I will exalt my throne above the stars of God; I will also sit on the mount of the congregation on the farthest sides of the north;
14 I will ascend above the heights of the clouds, I will be like the Most High.'
15 Yet you shall be brought down to Sheol, To the lowest depths of the Pit.

Scholars believe Isaiah 14:11-15 points to Lucifer. When you study him, he had many instruments built within him. Lucifer didn't just play instruments; he was a musical instrument. He was beautifully covered with gems, and when he moved, it was a spectacle of light and heavenly sound. Percussion wind and stringed instruments are all mentioned as being a part of him.

> *Ezekiel 28:12-13*
> [12] *"Son of man, take up a lamentation for the king of Tyre, and say to him,*
> *'Thus says the Lord GOD: "You were the seal of perfection,*
> *Full of wisdom and perfect in beauty.*
> [13] *You were in Eden, the garden of God;*
> *Every precious stone was your covering:*
> *The sardius, topaz, and diamond, Beryl, onyx, and jasper, Sapphire, turquoise,*
> *and emerald with gold. The workmanship of your timbrels and pipes*
> *Was prepared for you on the day you were created.*

I think it's interesting that the throne of God was surrounded by or covered by musical instruments. It's is obvious from these scriptures in Ezekiel 28 that music is incredibly important in the kingdom of God. Lucifer must've been a magnificent angel that led a gigantic orchestra and choir in heaven, leading a beautiful sound that would go on and on in the throne room. He understands music more than anything else because he was the original praise and worship leader in heaven. Music was his thing, and when he rebelled against God and was cast out of heaven, he took a third of the angels with him. We now know them as fallen angels or demons. This is why the battle over musicians and their lives is so strong. Music was created by God and for God to give Him honor and glory. But when Lucifer fell, he took the gift of music with him. And now it is twisted and used by the enemy to lead many people astray.

> *Isaiah 14:12-13*
> [12] *"How you are fallen from heaven, O Lucifer, son of the morning!*
> *How you are cut down to the ground, You who weakened the nations!*

Lucifer is weakening nations even today. Lucifer was beautiful and talented; his downfall was his arrogance and his desire to be worshiped. This arrogance opened the door for him to be deceived.

Warning to Anointed Worship Leaders

Let me just talk a moment here about talented and called musicians. If you're talented and if God has a call on your life, at some point you're going to be approached by others who would like to take your gift in another direction. Great music makes a lot of money. The music industry is driven by greed. Promoters, producers, and writers all make money off talented musicians. And they will try to take a talented, anointed musician and take them in another direction that exalts or glorifies the person and the gift, not God. This deception isn't anything new. It's been going on for thousands of years. The enemy wants to take your greatest strength and your greatest gift and use it to destroy you. He will set you up to be successful and rich and then when you think you've arrived, he will crush you. That's how he operates; he comes to steal, kill and destroy your life (John 10:10). Lucifer was beautiful, but God had to deal with him.

Ezekiel 28:15-16
15 You were perfect in your ways from the day you were created,
Till iniquity was found in you.
16 "By the abundance of your trading You became filled with violence within,
And you sinned; Therefore I cast you as a profane thing Out of the mountain of God;
And I destroyed you, O covering cherub, From the midst of the fiery stones.

Notice how the Scripture in Ezekiel 28:16 refers to "the abundance of your trading." Money is very seductive. Many people sell their souls for fame and fortune. This deception isn't anything new. There is going to be a spiritual battle over anyone who carries an anointing. The anointing of God will open doors for you and take you places that no one can imagine. But because of that, the enemy would like to destroy you because of the anointing you carry.

> *Revelation 12:7-9*
> *⁷ And war broke out in heaven: Michael and his angels fought with the dragon;*
> *and the dragon and his angels fought,*
> *⁸ but they did not prevail, nor was a place found for them in heaven any longer.*
> *⁹ So the great dragon was cast out, that serpent of old,*
> *called the Devil and Satan,*
> *who deceives the whole world; he was cast to the earth, and his angels*
> *were cast out with him.*
>
> *Revelation 12:4*
> *His tail drew a third of the stars of heaven and threw them to the earth.*

Man, however, was created to do something else. He was created to dominate and to demonstrate Satan's defeat on this earth. God created man to be next to Him. God uses man and flows through man, and God reigns through him on earth. We the believers are now the body of Christ. We are also known as the church. We believers are composed of men and women who stand with God and are filled with the Holy Spirit. We will stand in the last days to give God the worship and honor and glory He so deserves. We are His body.

> *Ephesians 1:19-23*
>
> *19 and what is the exceeding greatness of His power toward us who believe,*
> *according to the working of His mighty power*
> *20 which He worked in Christ when He raised Him from the dead*
> *and seated Him at His right hand in the heavenly places,*
> *21 far above all principality and power and might and dominion, and every*
> *name that is named, not only in this age but also in that which is to come.*
> *22 And He put all things under His feet, and gave Him to be head over all*
> *things to the church,*
> *23 which is His body, the fullness of Him who fills all in all.*

When Satan fell, his gift became perverted. These instruments of worship go all the way back to Cain. When you listen to music, what kind of atmosphere does it set? God is the author of peace, not of confusion. Any time you sense confusion in music, you might want to look at where that music is coming from.

1 Corinthians 14:33
For God is not the author of confusion but of peace, as in all the
churches of the saints.

Many times in Scripture we see the children of Israel being sucked into idolatry. We are not to worship anything but God. In the book of Exodus, we know the children of Israel were enticed and worshiping the golden calf. God dealt with this when he appeared in the burning Bush to Moses and announced that he was "I am that I am." They were worshiping the wrong thing. We see the same principle being set up in the book of Daniel. King Nebuchadnezzar would use musical instruments of all kinds to induce worship of an image that he created.

Daniel 3:7
So at that time, when all the people heard the sound of the horn, flute,
harp, and lyre,
in symphony with all kinds of music, all the people, nations, and languages
fell down and worshiped the gold image
which King Nebuchadnezzar had set up.

Music can set up the atmosphere for anything, including idol worship. You have to be very careful what you're glorifying or what the music you're singing is encouraging. We see this very clearly in the life of Jesus Christ. In his greatest example of prayer to his disciples, He said that we were to pray that God's will would be done on earth as it is in heaven. So the question is, what is God's will in heaven? What is being done in heaven now?

Heaven's Worship

We can learn a lot about heaven from the Book of Revelation. I love teaching from the Book of Revelation, and chapter four is one of my favorite chapters. It is a picture of the throne room of God. I love to pass out paper and markers and have my students sit down and draw what heaven looks like. It's a very interesting study. According to scripture, heaven is a noisy, active, musical place where worship and praise are going on at all times. When musicians write praise and worship songs based on this portion of scripture, they naturally carry an anointing. Kari Jobe made this portion of Scripture famous through her *Revelation* song. This song was so beautifully written that it reflects what's going on in heaven and what is being sung in heaven.

> *Revelation 4:8-11*
> *8 The four living creatures, each having six wings, were full of eyes around and within.*
> *And they do not rest day or night, saying: "Holy, holy, holy, Lord God Almighty,*
> *Who was and is and is to come!"*
> *9 Whenever the living creatures give glory and honor and thanks to Him who sits on the throne, who lives forever and ever,*
> *10 the twenty-four elders fall down before Him who sits on the throne and worship Him who lives forever and ever, and cast their crowns before the throne, saying:*
> *11 "You are worthy, O Lord, To receive glory and honor and power; For You created all things, And by Your will they exist and were created."*

I love this portion of Scripture because the 24 elders fall down and worship God at His throne. They bow before him and cast their crowns at his feet. Their crowns are symbols of their leadership or authority. It makes sense that these would be the 12 apostles and the 12 tribes of Israel. Later on in the Book of Revelation we learn about all the angels worshiping and praising God. There are a lot of them, so the worship in heaven must be loud and passionate.

> *Revelation 5:11-14*
> *11 Then I looked, and I heard the voice of many angels around the throne, the living creatures, and the elders; and the number of them was ten thousand times ten thousand, and thousands of thousands,*
> *12 saying with a loud voice: "Worthy is the Lamb who was slain To receive power and riches and wisdom, And strength and honor and glory and blessing!"*
> *13 And every creature which is in heaven and on the earth and under the earth and such as are in the sea, and all that are in them, I heard saying:*
> *"Blessing and honor and glory and power Be to Him who sits on the throne,*

> *And to the Lamb, forever and ever!"*
> *14 Then the four living creatures said, "Amen!" And the twenty-four elders*
> *fell down and worshiped Him who lives forever and ever.*

Since God's will is to be done on earth as it is in heaven, don't you think it's logical that we should worship God on earth? If that's what's happening in the throne room before God at all times, how much more should we worship God here on earth?

John was the disciple whom Jesus loved. When the Romans couldn't get him to be quiet and to stop sharing about Jesus, they tried to kill him by putting him into boiling oil. That didn't work, so they exiled him to the island of Patmos where he received his revelations. These revelations were written on scrolls and sent to the seven churches. John is the one who possibly lived a long life.

During this season on the Isle of Patmos, he had a series of visions in which he saw heaven. And the study of these visions is quite exciting. He saw people from every tribe and nation and tongue worshiping and praising God. They had palm branches in their hands, which is a symbol for the presence of God according to Jewish tradition.

> *Revelation 7:9-12*
> *9 After these things I looked, and behold, a great multitude which no one could number, of all nations, tribes, peoples, and tongues, standing before the throne and before the Lamb, clothed with white robes,*
> *with palm branches in their hands,*
> *10 and crying out with a loud voice, saying, "Salvation belongs to our God who sits on the throne, and to the Lamb!"*
> *11 All the angels stood around the throne and the elders and the four living creatures, and fell on their faces before the throne and worshiped God,*
> *12 saying: "Amen! Blessing and glory and wisdom, Thanksgiving and honor and power and might, Be to our God forever and ever. Amen."*

I love this vision of heaven. It's one of diversity and loud, passionate worship. This worship was creating new songs before God. There's nothing more enjoyable than hanging out with a group of musicians that create spontaneous songs for God. These spiritual songs come out of the spirit man. And because you're skillfully trained as a musician, you can figure out the chord structure. There is an example of this in Revelation 14:3 and it's truly beautiful.

Revelation 14:1-3
1 Then I looked, and behold, a Lamb standing on Mount Zion, and with Him one hundred and forty-four thousand, having His Father's name written on their foreheads.
2 And I heard a voice from heaven, like the voice of many waters, and like the voice of loud thunder. And I heard the sound of harpists playing their harps.
3 They sang as it were a new song before the throne, before the four living creatures, and the elders; and no one could learn that song except the hundred and forty-four thousand who were redeemed from the earth.

These 144,000 were redeemed from the earth and came from the 12 tribes of Israel. These were Jewish musicians who love to worship God. John sees this vision during the great tribulation time when the saints are joining together to worship Jesus after the destruction of Satan.

Revelation 15:2-4
2 And I saw something like a sea of glass mingled with fire, and those who have the victory over the beast, over his image and over his mark and over the number of his name, standing on the sea of glass, having harps of God.
3 They sing the song of Moses, the servant of God, and the song of the Lamb, saying: "Great and marvelous are Your works, Lord God Almighty! Just and true are Your ways, O King of the saints!
4 Who shall not fear You, O Lord, and glorify Your name? For You alone are holy. For all nations shall come and worship before You, For Your judgments have been manifested."

They are singing in heaven and worshiping God because they are watching what was prophesied take place. God is a just God. During this time, life on earth as we know it will be very difficult, but God has a plan. This plan is that there will be a new birth and earth will be restored and we will live in harmony with man and with God.

I think it's fascinating how men and women in heaven watch what's happening on earth, and they worship Him in the midst of it. It will be a dark season on the earth at that time. But when Satan is bound for 1,000 years, life on earth will be restored.

Revelation 19:1-2
After these things I heard a loud voice of a great multitude in heaven, saying,
"Alleluia! Salvation and glory and honor and power
belong
to the Lord our God!
2 For true and righteous are His judgments, because He has judged the great
harlot who corrupted the earth with her fornication; and He has avenged on her
the blood of His servants shed by her."
Again they said, "Alleluia! Her smoke rises up forever and ever!"

Revelation 19:7
Let us be glad and rejoice and give Him glory,
for the marriage of the Lamb has come,

We're the bride of Christ. We're going to be joined with Him. We are to prepare to meet Him, but we've got to make ourselves ready. Living a life of a vibrant musician serving the Lord is rewarding. But I hope that one day those of us who have led worship on earth will have the opportunity to lead worship in heaven. In fact, maybe we will be in charge of organizing worship in heaven. One thing we know for sure, worship is an important part of what we will be doing in eternity. Worship is eternal. It is holy.

Praise and worship isn't about our gifts; it's about preparing the body or the bride to meet her groom. Everything that we do should honor and glorify Him.

Revelation 22:20
He who testifies to these things says,
"Surely I am coming quickly." Amen.
Even so, come, Lord Jesus!

ABOUT THE AUTHOR

LeAnne Freesemann is a wife and a mom first. However, put a Bible in her hand and a song in her heart and you'll see why students of all ages look forward to being in her Bible and Music Ministry classes each year.

A graduate of Oral Roberts University, LeAnne holds a B.A. in Music Education and a minor in Musical Theater. She loves nothing more than to serve her students and friends through teaching. LeAnne taught secondary music at Victory Christian School in Tulsa, Okla. for 28 years and has award-winning choirs, bands and ensembles and continues to teach today. She considers it a privilege to serve young people from every denomination and culture. She wants each student to know the truths of Scripture intellectually by encouraging them to experience these truths practically by the power of the Holy Spirit.

In addition to LeAnne's extensive teaching experience, her passion is to study, teach, and write Christian books to help future leaders. LeAnne has had several students go on to pioneer churches and missions organizations throughout the United States and elsewhere. She has students who have won Dove Music Awards and have been successful in Christian Ministries. LeAnne's husband Grant graduated from Rhema Bible Training Center and PAM Bible School with Pam Vinnett. He has ministered in various groups, churches and conferences. He has traveled internationally and can relate to all types of men everywhere. LeAnne enjoys the honor of doing music ministry alongside her husband.

LeAnne has been married to Grant Freesemann for 29 years. Between studying and teaching, she spends most of her time helping her two ambitious kids. Jenava is a graduate from Oral Roberts University with a degree in Public Relations. She is an Internet marketing specialist and is married to Sean Ostrander. They both lead worship at their home church in Houston, Texas. Josiah is a Business Administration graduate from ORU and specializes in Human Relations.

They both love the Lord, and she counts that as her greatest success.

Attention colleges, universities, Bible colleges, churches or youth groups: Quantity discounts are available on bulk purchases of this book for education, training, or ministry purposes. Special books, booklets, or book excerpts can be created to fit your purposes or specific needs. For information, please contact the Author through www.restoringword.com.